MW00800595

Brett Miller

It's a Beautiful Day to Save Lives

A Medic's Journey
to His Destiny

authorHOUSE®

AuthorHouse™
1663 Liberty Drive
Bloomington, IN 47403
www.authorhouse.com
Phone: 833-262-8899

© 2021 Brett Miller. All rights reserved.

No part of this book may be reproduced, stored in a retrieval system, or transmitted by any means without the written permission of the author.

Published by AuthorHouse 05/05/2021

ISBN: 978-1-6655-2466-7 (sc)
ISBN: 978-1-6655-2465-0 (hc)
ISBN: 978-1-6655-2464-3 (e)

Library of Congress Control Number: 2021908934

Print information available on the last page.

Any people depicted in stock imagery provided by Getty Images are models, and such images are being used for illustrative purposes only.
Certain stock imagery © Getty Images.

This book is printed on acid-free paper.

Because of the dynamic nature of the Internet, any web addresses or links contained in this book may have changed since publication and may no longer be valid. The views expressed in this work are solely those of the author and do not necessarily reflect the views of the publisher, and the publisher hereby disclaims any responsibility for them.

To all who are or may be in the struggle to save themselves
or others, and to my family and dear friends in the
hopes they will better understand who I am.

There is no greater agony than bearing an untold story inside you.

—Maya Angelou

THE
COMBAT MEDIC PRAYER

Oh Lord, I ask for the divine strength
to meet the demands of my profession.
Help me to be the finest medic,
both technically and tactically.
If I am called to the battlefield,
give me the courage to conserve our
fighting forces by providing medical
care to all who are in need.
If I am called to a mission of peace,
give me the strength to lead by caring for
those who need my assistance.
Finally, Lord help me take care
of my own spiritual, physical
and emotional needs.
Teach me to trust in your
presence and never-failing love.

AMEN

Contents

Contents

Chapter 1

Plane Ride to Life

" W OULD ANYONE WITH MEDICAL EXPERIENCE please come to the front of the plane right away."

After a millisecond of blank stares from people waiting and wondering if anyone would stand up or speak up, I rose from my seat and briskly walked to the front of the plane. There, I found a young man with his hand over his chest sitting in the flight attendant's seat. His head was bent down, his face in a grimace.

This can't be good, I thought.

He was tucked away at the front of first class near the cockpit. He was sweating and pale, and he looked very afraid. I shifted gears from relaxing in the back of the plane and accessed my organic hard drive that stored my emergency medicine files with all the signs, symptoms, and results of what I was seeing. The first-class flight attendant continued her business as usual and asked me occasionally if I needed anything.

I found out his name was Dan, and I began rifling questions at him as I did a physical assessment. "Do you have high blood pressure?"

"No."

"Are you having any left arm tingling or jaw pain?"

"No."

"Do you take any medications?"

"No."

"On a scale of zero to ten, rate the chest pain you're feeling right now."

"Eight."

Whoa. That was not a good number.

Using the art of distraction—a good way to get a patient to calm down a bit—I asked him what he did for work and why he was flying to Los Angeles.

He seemed to be a gentle man and was very soft spoken. I found out that he was an EMT in a suburb of Boston and was flying to LA to see his niece graduate from nursery school. He told me that he had had a regular morning—drank a few cups of coffee, had breakfast—and that this had never happened to him before. He exercised three days a week and worked full time but understood that like most of us, he could lose a few pounds. He was only thirty-four and had no medical or family history that would raise alarms. In fact, a few days earlier, his primary care doctor had given him a physical with a normal EKG and good report.

But something clearly was going on with his body despite the clear doctor visit. That something looked to be cardiac in nature or stress related.

And with his high heart rate, high blood pressure, diaphoresis—clammy skin and perspiration on his face and skin—and a subjective report of chest pain he ranked eight out of ten, I knew that despite the recent doctor's report, this man was in trouble.

It was June 1, 2019, a beautiful morning with bright sun and not a cloud in the sky—a perfect day to fly. I had boarded the plane at Logan International in Boston and was heading for LA. I was working with an amazing company that had been doing research on Parkinson's disease technology. Knowing that I had a five-hour flight, I'd set up my workstation in my roomy plane seat with my laptop propped on the tray table; I had planned to catch up on some work. I had so many new ideas and innovative projects to launch for the business I had started a year and a half earlier. I had launched 110 Fitness in January 2018, and it had quickly morphed into not only the largest wellness center in the world for people with Parkinson's disease but also an inclusive wellness center for people of all abilities and disabilities including adults, youth, and disabled veterans.

I guessed that most people on the plane that day considered it an inconvenience when they heard the announcement from the cockpit and thought that their travel plans might be interrupted. For me, however, it was no surprise to be called into action again. In fact, it was meant to happen—It was one more call from the universe for me to fulfill my destiny of saving lives.

I was surprised to learn that most commercial flights carry an array of medical equipment, medicine, and supplies. I was used to flying in military helicopters and being very limited with what I had to offer the sick and wounded. When I asked the flight attendant for any medical supplies, she opened multiple drawers and handed me three large bags wrapped in plastic. Each item in the bags were wrapped in plastic and labeled in detail. She also reached into a drawer and handed me a stethoscope and a small bottle of oxygen with tubing that could be used as a nasal cannula—tubing that can be put into someone's nose to deliver the oxygen.

Luckily for Dan that day, his seat was the window seat of the first row of first class; that gave me room to work. I got him back to the aisle seat in his row and reclined him as far as possible in case I needed to do CPR and use the defibrillator. I dug through the large plastic bags with labeled medical supplies and found and immediately administered a sublingual nitroglycerin.

Document the time, Miller, I reminded myself.

I instinctively knew Dan's chest pain wasn't going away easily. I found an automatic blood pressure cuff for the bicep and a pulse oximeter, and though Dan was oxygenating at 97 percent, his pulse was over a hundred at rest, and his blood pressure was high. Not a great combination at thirty thousand feet.

Due to the nature of the pain and the fact that it wasn't subsiding, Dan was frightened. Because he was an EMT, he knew the consequences of his symptoms as well as about being unable to receive extensive medical care on a plane. He was very fidgety and was very quiet.

Eight minutes after the nitroglycerin, Dan reported that his chest pain had decreased but that his pain was moving below the left side of his chest and slightly down into his abdomen. At that point, we were flying over the Midwest along the Great Lakes.

The captain came out of the cockpit and looked us over. "Do we need to land right away in Cleveland, or can we push on? We can land at Chicago O'Hare if necessary."

My biggest concern was the time frame between the stops in case something emergent happened and we needed to land right away.

Dan spoke up. "I think I might just be having some anxiety. Or maybe a GI problem. A gas bubble or indigestion?" He sounded unsure of course.

We jointly decided to keep flying at that point, and the captain let us know that Colorado would be the next possible emergency landing option. Colorado was another hour of flight away, which would seem like an eternity while you were sitting next to someone with chest pain and monitoring vitals and checking in with every ten minutes or so.

I continued to monitor Dan and tried to distract him from his anxiety and discomfort while keeping the flight attendant up to speed on his progress. I had her rummage through the plane for all the medical supplies available. I wanted to know what I had and that it was accessible to me in a moment's notice just in case things went south quickly. As they often reminded us in the US Army noncommissioned officer school, piss-poor planning equaled piss-poor performance. That resonated with me many times that day.

I alternated between standing over him and sitting on the armrest of the seat next to him. Suddenly, I saw Dan twist in the seat and go fully upright moaning with discomfort.

"What's wrong?" I asked calmly.

"It's a sharp pain in my chest!" He clutched at himself just below his breast line and gasped.

"Open your mouth," I said; I popped another nitro under his tongue; I monitored his vitals. It had been about only twenty minutes since his first dose, and I knew that if this second dose didn't help, we would need to get this bird on the ground right away.

I gathered all my supplies and asked the folks on the opposite side of the plane to move so I could be ready for anything. Flashbacks to 1996 when I was serving as a combat medic in the army during the Bosnian crisis played over and over in my mind, and my reactions and responses were high speed and focused.

I put oxygen via a nasal cannula on Dan, and his vitals started to level out. He rested for the next hour and was able to maintain steady vitals. I was in constant contact with the captain, flight attendant, and medical doctors on the ground via the cockpit radio that I used through the flight attendant's phone. Regardless of Dan's stability at the moment, we collectively decided that we were making a landing in Denver about forty-five minutes away at that point. Whether we emergency landed or not, this guy was going to a hospital sooner rather than later.

I told the doctors on the ground, "I'm prepping to place an IV." Dan needed some fluids, and I needed access. I continued to be amazed at the plane's array of medical supplies including a 16-gauge needle and IV setup. Dan was on a second tank of oxygen, and I was looking for something to improvise as a tourniquet; it would be very difficult for me to hit the vein on the first attempt without one. I also needed some way to hang up a bag of fluid. I felt the universe remind me, *You got this, Miller. Improvise and adapt. It's a beautiful day to save lives. You were born for this. It's your destiny.*

I felt intact and sharp, like being in the field. I arranged my supplies, used the blood pressure cuff as a tourniquet, and borrowed a long computer Velcro strap from a passenger to create a hanger for the saline. Dan and I agreed it was time to place the IV and to land, whatever the outcome might be.

As I pumped up the blood pressure cuff, despite any dehydration issues with his veins, I saw a lump protruding from the left center of the inside of his elbow. I gently placed my thumb on the distal portion of the vein for stability and to make sure it wouldn't roll as I inserted the needle into his arm.

Bang! Nailed it the first time and opened that tubing like a running faucet. Hung the bag off the overhead bin with the Velcro, and we were in business. It had been a long time since I had placed an IV, but I prided myself on always being a prepared soldier no matter the situation. I have lived my life by this mantra, and it served me well there.

As Murphy's law would have it, when we were just about thirty minutes from Denver, Dan reported an increase in his chest pain and started having what looked like quick, short bouts of passing out. I called the captain to expedite a landing. Within seconds, the message came over the intercom: "Please take your seats, stow your tray tables, and buckle your seat belts. Due to a medical emergency, we will be landing immediately."

The plane dropped suddenly, and I felt a quick sensation of floating and an emptiness in my stomach. I don't think I had ever dropped out of the sky that fast accept for the times I was wearing a parachute.

The flight attendant said, "Brett, the FAA requires all passengers to be in their seats and buckled in order for the plane to land." I squared away Dan's equipment, took one last set of vitals, and leaned over to reassure him. "I'll be back up here to get you off the plane when we land. And I'll report to the EMTs."

I noted Dan's nervousness and headed back many rows; I had been sitting in the rear of that big old jet. Within minutes, *Boom!* We hit the tarmac, and the plane decelerated. As soon as the plane was stable, I jumped up and briskly walked forward to check on Dan and prepare for his departure from the plane. Dan had some semblance of relief—physical and emotional alike—since we had touched soil. I took another quick set of vitals for my report to the first responders as we were taxiing.

The plane stopped. Two paramedics along with some security and fire officials clambered onboard and began asking questions.

I gave them the situation report. "He started with some significant chest pain that responded well to nitroglycerin times two twenty minutes apart. I was able to stabilize his vitals, but as soon as his symptoms started to increase, we opted for the emergency landing and I placed the IV so that you folks would have access."

That info would help them expedite his care on the way to the hospital. I saw Dan's face relax and his body ease somewhat knowing that he was on the ground and that medical help was on its way. The paramedics quickly put him on a stretcher and were already in their groove with questions and checking vitals.

"Goodbye and good luck!" I waved to Dan as he was trundled off the plane. We then turned back down the runway to head for LA.

I took my seat and reflected on what had just happened. I knew I had done all I could have to keep Dan safe that day, and I knew he would be well once he made it to the hospital and received further care.

I was grateful for my army training as a combat medic ready to do what was necessary by being prepared mentally and physically.

I think of Dan often and hope to see him someday. I'll remind him that it was a beautiful day to save lives and that the universe had plans for us. I'm sure he was grateful that I had marched up the aisle that beautiful day in June to help him. For me, it was no surprise that I had been on that plane. As a matter of fact, I believe it had been planned.

Chapter 2

The Cranberry Bogs Come Alive

I T ALL STARTED FOR ME at age six. The universe's plan rolled out unannounced.

I grew up in Norwell, a small, rural town on the South Shore of Massachusetts. In 1976, when I was four, we moved there after my mom divorced my dad. I had one brother, Kerry, who was four years older. We pretty much hung out together day and night because my mom was always working to make ends meet. She was a certified nursing assistant who worked in nursing homes and whenever she could in private homes helping taking care of elderly folks. We were poor, but we enjoyed what we had. We were very lucky that my grandfather babysat us some days while my mom worked. Unfortunately, all too often, I found myself standing looking out the bay window and crying because my mom was driving off to work again as my poor grandfather tried to console me.

Back then, Mom wore nursing whites that were always covered with food, urine, feces, and vomit (*Yeehaw!*). She lifted heavy patients, gave people bed baths, and performed other types of personal care for them. Her clothes after work always had that nursing home scent—a little mothball mixed with that old-people smell—distinct and recognizable.

The seventies were a great time to be a kid. Nerf flying toys, Big Wheels, dominoes, and cards dominated our home life. We ate chunky soup, chipped beef, corned beef hash, baked beans, and brown bread all from cans. We watched scads of television on only three stations including *Superfriends*, *Tom and Jerry*, and *Mister Rogers' Neighborhood*. We played outside unsupervised for hours and hours. The hot cars were

Chevy Camaros, Ford Mustangs, and the GM muscle cars; the cold cars were AMC Matador station wagons and any Chrysler product. It's a cliché to say so, but it was truly a more innocent time.

Norwell was a beautiful farm town back then; only a few hundred people lived there. The center of town was quaint and had a fire and police station, town hall, post office, a small family restaurant, and a convenience store. It was like something out of a television show I realize now.

We lived way down a long, one-way dirt road unkept and full of large potholes and puddles on a run-down boat marina called King's Landing. It was a peaceful marina—not much if any traffic and surrounded by woods. We had a small, one-level house with a nice yard. My mom did her best to provide for us after she left my dad, but wore the fatigue on her face.

The marina was owned by the Lincolns, a family well known in town for having some issues with alcohol. Mr. Lincoln used to walk up and down our dirt road daily mumbling to himself and usually with his shotgun in hand, and it was a contest between my brother and me to see who could run the fastest from riding our Big Wheels in the driveway to a safe hiding spot before he staggered by the house.

"Here comes Mr. Lincoln! Run!"

We knew he was harmless, but part of us was really scared. King's Landing was where the poor people lived, and only four or five other run-down homes stood on the road, but it gave us an opportunity to live in a nice town and have lots of freedom to roam in the woods and the boatyard, and it gave my mom a place to keep her kids engaged, busy, and growing up in a wholesome environment.

About a year or so after moving there, my mom met a wonderful man who became the father we didn't have. His name was Howie, and he owned a shoe store in Hingham, another beautiful, rural town similar to Norwell on the South Shore about twenty minutes from where we lived. He also worked part time for the Hingham Police Department.

Howie was a hard-working man; he worked six days a week and always helped my mom with house maintenance, bath times, meals, and bed time. He was very different from my biological father, who really wasn't around at all. Howie was a lean man with a nice mustache, glasses, and thinning black hair—friendly, strong, and deeply in love with my mom.

Howie also worked nights as a security guard for a construction site, and we would often visit him and take him hot meals with my mom. He encouraged us to help him with projects for the house and was always very patient teaching us life skills. Our family was blessed to have him. Although my brother and I initially had a very hard time accepting a new father figure, Howie showed us stability as a provider and genuine love for my mom as a partner.

In the summer of 1978—I was almost seven—Howie had been living with us for a year and he had asked my mom to be his lifelong partner in marriage. I don't remember any discussion with my mom about our thoughts as kids, but it was understood that Howie was our hero and what we needed to make a better life for us all.

It was a quaint wedding with all my mom's and dad's close friends at the United Church of Christ in Norwell performed by the minister, David Norling, who was loved by the community. As the ring bearer, I proudly walking down the aisle with my seventies-style peach and brown three-piece suit holding a small pillow with the rings.

"Keep the rings on the pillow, Brett, smile, and walk slowly," various people told me. "You're going to do great."

Howie had two sons from a previous marriage, who were also in the wedding, and that made us a family of four boys ranging in age from six to the midtwenties. Howie was twenty years older than my mom.

My brother and I soon found ourselves in the clerk magistrate's office adopting Howie's last name, Miller. We were no longer Raymonds of the famous paint store in Scituate, Massachusetts, Raymond's Paints. That was my dad's family business for many years and how people related to us as young kids. Writing a different last name in school took some getting used to, but it eventually became second nature.

Life looked brighter for us Raymonds—now Millers—in the winter of 1978. My mom and new dad found the home of their dreams in Norwell on beautiful cranberry bogs on Cross Street. It was way out of their price range at $42,000, but they were going to make it work not only for them but also for my brother, Kerry, and me, the only two siblings still at home.

We moved into 254 Cross Street. We had our own bedrooms on the second floor with two bathrooms. We had a basement, and our backyard went on across the cranberry bogs as far as the eye could see. Dirt sand roads circled each bog that had a moat of water with tall pines and typically a blueberry patch. Wildlife settled near bogs, fish and frogs were in all the water sources, and snakes, snapping turtles, hawks galore, and more rarely, wood ducks and fisher cats made up the animal population. In the winter, it was a huge, barren, open space. A harsh wind often covered it in snow. The blueberry patch leaves turned a dull brown, and the tall pine trees swung in the breeze like long matchsticks.

In winter, kids ice-skated on the frozen bogs, played hockey, and drank hot cocoa around a small fire. We didn't own ice skates, but my brother and I walked down to the ice and slid around like kids who had never seen ice before. We loved our new house.

The blizzard of 1978 made the record books. For most people in the area, especially those living on the South Shore, it was a catastrophic storm with about a hundred fatalities and five thousand injured. Boston had a record-breaking snowfall of 27.1 inches. The storm surprised many, and back in those days, we lacked any significant warning of its severity. More than 3,500 cars were abandoned on the highway. Due to the tide cycles, some of the worst coastal flooding ever recorded occurred. People were without homes, power, food, and water for weeks. Wind gusts of 110 mph were recorded in nearby Scituate.

The storm brought snow piled well over my head, and we were without power for weeks, but Kerry and I were in our glory sledding, building tunnels, and walking to the convenience store with my parents for milk and bread and of course a piece of candy. My parents? Well, not so much fun for them. Shoveling snow daily and figuring out meals and how to stay warm were their games, but they played them well.

Kerry was long, very tall, and as skinny as a rail. I was short and stout. Of course I looked up to him literally and figuratively as most younger siblings do. Four years is a pretty significant age difference in kids, and Kerry was ahead me in physical stature, school, and education. We tussled as all brothers do, but we loved each other.

After the storm cleared and we got back to our routine, it was time to shovel a perfect square on the ice for our hockey rink and explore our backyard winter wonderland. My parents found a way to buy used skates, two hockey sticks, and a puck from the Salvation Army for Christmas. We played every day after school and every weekend whether the ice was smooth or bumpy, snow-covered or not. We spent half our childhood on that ice playing street against street and town against town. The only rule was no open slap shots; otherwise, it was game on! Some days we won, and some days we learned. It was a beautiful time for making friends and making a few enemies but mostly for making great memories.

February 5, 1978, was a crisp winter Sunday, and the sun shone brightly. I smelled that perfect scent of winter as it burned through my nostrils from the cold. Kerry and I decided to head out on a cranberry bog adventure. Being a Sunday afternoon, we wanted one more adventure for the weekend before heading back to school on Monday. We always dreaded Sunday afternoons and evenings because we knew we had to go back to school the next day.

The bogs were flooded in the winter, and the water was typically about two to three feet deep when frozen except around the edges, where there was a canal, but it did not exceed four feet in depth. Cranberry bogs naturally need a water source, and ours was a giant pond about three hundred yards from the house. It was tucked in the back corner of the bog property and was surrounded on two sides by trees and woods. We spent our summers swimming and fishing there, but we never played on the ice because we knew it was very deep and wouldn't freeze all the way down. Due to the typical heavy winds across the cranberry bogs in winter, the snow would drift around. The ice depth could be anywhere from a couple of inches to a couple of feet; you never could really tell by just looking at it.

This pond had jagged stumps and old logs sticking up from it that had been there for years, since it was first constructed, which also made it difficult to tell whether the ice was thick enough to be on.

It had been a long, cold winter with many weeks of below-freezing temps at night. The ice was thick, and Kerry and I thought it would be a great revenge on those stumps to recollect our fishing lures we had so frustratingly lost when they had snagged on those stumps during the summer days. We tromped through the thick snow and headed way out back by the outer edge of the bogs along the tree line to the pond far back from our house. Out of breath from the long walk in deep snow, we planned our attack remembering where we had lost the most gear before setting out onto the bog pond ice.

We slowly edged out onto the ice since we were experienced bog testers; we banged our feet and jumped up and down to test the thickness of the ice. There was a lot of air bubbles and pockets in the ice that day, so I really couldn't see through the ice into the depths of the pond. It was a cloudy white color with random spots of black.

"Perfect!" I said. "It's good. Let's collect our lures!"

It was like getting new fishing gear all over again as we pulled back and forth on those treble hooks that had snagged on the stumps. We triumphantly put them in our pockets.

We had never been on that pond in the winter; it was creepy and kind of tucked in the back corner of the bogs seemingly separate from everything and everyone. We felt like Lewis and Clark discovering uncharted territory and couldn't wait to tell our friends about it.

Kerry and I were running and sliding across the pond as far as we could go getting our "lasties" in when we decided we'd had our fill. It was getting dark and time to head home. We started scrambling to the edge of the pond when I heard a crack and the ice started breaking behind me. My brother had disappeared.

Kerry gave a quick gasp of fear and surprise; he had no time to yell. He had fallen through the ice. I couldn't see him. With all the air bubbles, the ice was white, and he was underneath it somewhere, but I couldn't find him. My heart was pounding. I was frantically trying to respond to the situation but was frozen myself.

The hole in the ice was just big enough for him to have fallen through. The water was deep blue and breathed cold just looking at it. The edges were cracked and sharp, bright white against the dark water. It looked like a black hole ready to swallow anything that dared to go near it. Unsafe. Scary. Deadly. I didn't want to get to close to the hole because I was afraid that I might fall in too.

To my shock, Kerry bounced up under the ice, about four feet from the hole. As he surfaced, I saw bubbles oozing out of his mouth. He frantically tried to bust through the ice. I saw his face as he came up only to hit the ice with his hand trying to break it, but then he was gone again. It felt like minutes had gone by due to my panic.

We're dead.

We knew we weren't supposed to play on that pond. What were we thinking? Why did I say the ice was perfect and good when I really didn't know? My mom was going to be pissed, and my dad, well, that was going to be worse.

In desperation, I grabbed a stump finger coming out of the ice and wrestled it loose. I kept shoving it into the hole like a spear fisherman over and over trying to break the hole open wider and hoping to find any part of Kerry I could touch. I thought he was gone and was about to give up. I dropped to my knees cold and wet wondering why I couldn't save him. Just then, I felt a tug on the stick. There was my brother coming up for air as if he were about to take his last breath.

I pulled him out of the hole slowly still afraid I might go in too. I was able to get him up only to his waist, and he rested on the jagged ice edge. He kicked frantically despite being physically exhausted. He tried to get more of his frozen body out of the hole. I lay down on my chest hoping to get any mechanical advantage at all until he was able to put a knee up on the ice edge. But even as careful as I was, as he inched out, I was being pulled in.

At one point, we looked at each other as brothers and for milliseconds walked the line between giving up or pressing on. With the grace of God in that moment, Kerry was able to press his hands down and slide on his belly across the ice as I pulled as hard as I could on his drenched parka dragging his body across the ice. He was frozen, heavy, hypothermic, and in shock from fear. So was I. Somehow, we managed to get out.

We slowly crawled to the pond's edge, gradually stood as we got close to land, and breathlessly recovered from what would have been a sad, clichéd, winter news story—"Two Boys Drown while Playing on Unsafe Ice."

I put his arm over my shoulder, and we walked home like two kids who had just had the life stripped out of them. My brother could barely walk because his pants and clothes were at that point frozen stiff, and he was shivering relentlessly from the cold. I kept checking in on him as we walked home in silence. I'm sure we were both wondering what had just happened and how we had managed to still be alive. We were just hoping we would make the journey back to our house. We knew that once my mom got over being hysterical from what could've happened, we were dead.

We sure paid the price that Saturday when my dad came home from work.

Mom cried and hugged us, but Dad clearly was angry. "You had zero business being out on that pond!" he yelled. "It was irresponsible, and you know it! Take off your wet clothes and put them by the fire!" He shook his head and walked away in disgust.

We never viewed that creepy pond the same way after that day whether we were fishing in the summer or skating nearby in the winter. It had lived up to its reputation of stealing fishing lure after fishing lure and had almost stolen my brother's life. It was that nightmare we all talk about of not being able to get air being submerged under something.

That night when I rested my head on my pillow grateful to be warm and dry, I felt good to have been the younger brother who had saved his older brother. I felt loyal to my family, and I felt proud. I'm not sure what happened that day, but I had responded when I didn't have a response, and that was the start of my journey.

It was a beautiful day to save lives.

The infamous scene of the crime

Skating on the cranberry bogs with Kerry (left) in 1982

King's Landing Marina in Norwell with Kerry

16

At the town hall in Norwell during the blizzard of 1978

A proud ring bearer

Chapter 3

A Bad Day at the Beach

I F YOU EVER LIVED IN New England and especially in Massachusetts in the seventies, you probably spent many summer days on Nantasket Beach and many summer nights at Paragon Park. It was a beautiful time to be alive.

I remember as a kid coming over that hill in the back of my dad's Chevy pickup headed into the town of Hull and seeing that amazing wooden roller-coaster towering over everything. Riders screaming with hands in the air and smiles from ear to ear. *Click, click, click, click* as the roller coaster climbed way up over the beautiful coastline. That millisecond of silence ... and *Vroom!* I hear the sounds today, and they're soothing to my soul. Smells of fried dough, cotton candy, and salty beachness filled the air. Kids running up and down the boulevard playing Skee-Ball and pinball shirtless with wet swimming bottoms. Riding the carousel with bare feet calloused from the summer's wear and tear chasing the last bit of sunlight.

My grandfather's family was from Hull; he lived on B Street for most of his life. On one of her rare days off, my mom would convince me to go visit her dad, my grandfather, by allowing me to swim at Nantasket Beach for a short time.

Mom was a thin, unassuming woman who worked really hard. She had been raised in Hull and had the privilege of spending her summers as a kid in Nantasket with folks like the Kennedy family. She was very fair and covered with freckles. She had long, red hair, and she suffered from a rare allergy to the sun, so our time at the beach was always limited. But if you grew up around Nantasket in the summer, it was the place to be especially at age seven because the waves were colossal during high tide; I body-surfed to my heart's content.

Nothing was different that day except that we picked up my close friend, Greg, on the way to the beach in the neighboring town of Cohasset. Greg was a quiet kid and didn't really have a big circle of friends. He was a fit, young boy who loved adventure as I did. He kept to himself, but once we were united by our parents for play dates and such, we were off to the races. Our moms had been friends since we were little, and we spent many days together as infants and into our youth.

We were psyched that day to be together. We loved the ocean and loved to swim especially in those huge waves. My mom never learned how to swim and naturally was afraid of water. I believe that it was because of that fear and handicap that she had put my brother and me in the water as soon as we could stand. She started us as toddlers at an indoor pool in Norwell.

So even at age seven, I was a strong swimmer, and she'd let my brother and me swim as she watched from her car trying to stay out of the sun. There were days when she dropped us off at the beach at nine with drinks and lunch, and she would pick us up at three. However, because Greg was with me and not as strong a swimmer, that day, she walked down onto the hot sand and waited for us in her overly wide, brimmed hat and holding an umbrella. It was a beautiful day—sun pouring down, peak high tide—and off we went running and diving headfirst into the first wave we could catch.

Greg and I were having the time of our life that day between the weather, good friendship, and the energy that made Nantasket so famous. That day, though, the waves seemed extra big as they pulled the sand and rocks into the depths and then came back to crash again. They were alive that day. I prayed not to get beaten by the rocks in the undertow while body-surfing.

We waded in as far as we could and positioned ourselves right for the wave's biggest peak but still able to touch the sandy bottom so we would have something to push off of. Just as a monster of a wave came, we threw our hands out in front of us, heads down, tucked chins, waiting to feel that explosion of momentum as we surfed across the surface of the wave taking us all the way to the shore. What a sensation of exhilaration and power. It was great fun for two kids at age seven living the best life.

My mom was at her limit with the sun, and we were exhausted from the constant back and forth riding the waves like pro body surfers. She called to us from the beach, "Five more minutes, boys, and then we have to leave. It's getting late."

"One more, Greg!" I shouted giddy with excitement and full of energy. "Let's go out and see if we can ride it the whole way in."

"Perfect," he said.

We went way out for that last ride, and what a ride it was. There were two colossal rollers coming in hot, and we negotiated with the ocean.

"Let's get this!"

"No! Let's wait."

"I'm going."

"OK, me too!"

Off we went pushing our feet up, heads down, and hands out on top of the crest for our best performance. Vying for the wave's attention as it vigorously moved us across its body fast and furious. Getting it all in for that last ride. Full of power and for a long time.

The ocean roared as it pushed me faster and faster as I got closer and closer to the shore. I reached down and felt the sand. I jumped up and was like, *Yes! What a last ride!* I was grinning with pure satisfaction. "Greg! I made it all the way!" I yelled as I looked next to me. But there was no Greg.

Startled, I paused. *Where's Greg? He'd been right next to me.* I looked left, I looked right, I waited for Greg to surface, and then I turned around and looked back at the horizon. The waves were just continuing to crash onto shore, but no Greg. I couldn't believe it. I looked up at the beach for my mom thinking maybe he had gotten ahead of me, but she was patiently waiting for us reading her book.

"Greg! Greg!" I ran back and forth in the shore waves, kicking my feet, hoping to feel him under the water and that he'd just come in from the wave. It seemed like forever.

I yelled for my mom, panicking. "Ma! I can't find Greg! I can't find Greg!"

She dropped her book and started to run to me, but I couldn't wait, and my mom couldn't swim. It was getting late in the day; there weren't many people hanging around the beach, so I made a decision. I ran to the water, dove in, and opened my eyes to that saltwater sting. Frantic, I looked all around for Greg. Everything was loud like being in a fishbowl, and everything was blurry because I couldn't focus due to the salt water stinging my eyes. I had to find him. I was going to drown finding him. I didn't care. I came up gasping for air. I couldn't hold my breath long because I was so afraid. I was full of fear, and my heart was thumping. There I was neck deep in the ocean getting pounded one wave after another trying to jump up to see if I could see Greg. Time was everything at that point.

I thought I saw a dark shadow right in front of me in one of the rollers. I plunged my hand into the eye of that wave, and it was Greg. I don't know what came over me, but I grabbed him by his shorts and dragged him to shore as fast as I could. Thank God for buoyancy because it was like pulling a dead fish out of the water. I'm sure my high level of adrenaline made that task thoughtless.

On the sand, I was huffing and wheezing and lifeless myself. Greg looked like a wet rag doll. He was choking and jerking and flailing his arms and legs. He threw up on the beach and slowly came back to life. Lying there staring at me exhausted and speechless.

My mom was always a very nervous person, and that situation amplified that persona. She came running down to the water line, where I had Greg in the sand, but she was relying on me to help Greg; she clearly didn't know what to do.

"Is he OK? What happened? Is he breathing? Are you OK? Do we need to go to the hospital?" The situation brought out her nervousness.

As Greg slowly started to catch his breath and come back to some sense of normal consciousness, I asked, "What happened, Greg? Where did you go?"

"I missed the first wave and got sucked under by the second wave and never recovered. I thought I was drowning and getting dragged out

21

to sea. I had no control and thought for sure I was going to drown." He started to cry in between his coughs.

"Let's just go home," I said.

It took Greg a good fifteen minutes to be able to walk to the car that day, and he still looked like he had seen a monster. He was wide eyed, silent, and scared. Exhausted, we all staggered to the car and jumped in. As we drove out of the parking lot, I looked back at the ocean. I didn't really know what to think except for the first time, I realized that the ocean was alive. Thinking back, I suspect he had probably been caught in some sort of a rip current, which Nantasket was known for, but we didn't know that then. To us, it felt like some sort of monster in the water, its power unseen yet felt. We didn't talk the whole car ride home. We were both still playing out in our minds what the hell had just happened and how we had made it out alive.

We never talked about that incident. Greg was never the same. When we went to the beach together after that, we stayed close to shore and always watched the water's behavior before going in. I respected his decision, and I certainly understood why.

That night like every night, my mom put me to bed after reading books; she reassured me that it was OK to be upset and scared still from such a traumatic event. I had been silent during that car ride home, at the dinner table, and right up until reading books. I couldn't believe what had happened. It was so surreal. I kept playing it over and over in my mind.

"Mom, I was really scared today," I finally admitted.

My mom replied positively as she always did. "Brett, you were very brave today, and you saved Greg's life. This is something that might be on your mind for a while, but remember to always be of service to people who need help."

I was emotionless that night; heroism wasn't even a thought at that point. I knew what I had to do in that ocean that day. I fell fast asleep from exhaustion and moved on with my life the next day as a typical seven-year-old would.

I think this was the unannounced universe putting things in place for my purpose here on earth and slowly engaging me at age seven for many days and many experiences to come.

August 1979 at Nantasket Beach was a beautiful day to save lives.

Nantasket Beach in Hull with Greg

Chapter 4

Geoff and the Trials of Recess

FIRST GRADE FOR MOST KIDS was their first time being in school all day, all week. In 1979, kindergarten was a half day, so my move up to first grade was a change that took some adjusting to, but it was a beautiful time to be alive, and I loved it. Academics at that point weren't so demanding, and I was able to sit in the back of a bus and goof around, have lunch with my schoolmates, and get recess two times a day with my friends. It was terrific.

Vinal School, nestled in the woods of Norwell, had a big circular driveway and windows all around for the benefit of us daydreamers. I lived near the school and often walked through the woods to school or rode my bike there. There weren't many people in my town and certainly not many cars on the road, so it was safe to travel there, and most of the time, my older brother, Kerry, would accompany me.

Mrs. Davis was the nicest person to have as a first-grade teacher; I thought she was the prettiest lady in the world, and she knew it. She had soft skin that was darker in complexion and short black hair. She was thin, and her big brown eyes complemented by a long smile were always happy to see her first graders.

I worked extra hard to get my schoolwork correct, and I raised my hand whenever I could to participate. Mrs. Davis respected my desire to participate and eagerness to learn, and I respected her. Plus, we were going to get married, right? The mind of a seven-year-old. Funny, isn't it?

Mrs. Davis respected one other boy in my class, Geoff, my best friend; he was as eager as I was to do well and participate in class. He lived on my street, which made it very convenient for play dates and bike rides. He was a meek and somewhat shy kid; he was skinny and had towhead blond hair. He was smart. It was the seventies, so we all wore weird, unmatched, plaid and stripe combinations of pants and shirts.

Life was simple then. After school, we would get off the bus at each other's houses to play or ride bikes home together. Some days, a whole crew of us would stay at school and bike ride around the school or play football and other games until it was almost dark. Now, that's termed free-range childhood; kids exploring and playing on their own was just the norm back then, and it was a blast. Our parents knew we were all together somewhere and were for the most part good kids staying out of trouble. Boy, we took those times for granted.

One day that fall, we played the game in class; someone started a story, and the others in turn told the story to the person to their right. We all heard how much it had changed by the time it came full circle.

Geoff had been dismissed from class that day for a doctor's appointment. I thought nothing of it initially, but the doctor's appointments became weekly events for about three weeks, and sometimes, Geoff didn't come to school at all. I would hop on the bus expecting to see my best friend who I'd last seen fourteen hours earlier to catch up with only to be let down by his absence.

"Geoff, why do you have all these doctor's appointments all of a sudden?" I asked him a few days later. "Are you sick? You're never in school anymore."

He replied very nonchalantly, "I'm fine. My mom scheduled a lot of appointments for regular checkups at the same time, you know, the dentist and my physical."

Because of his dismissive attitude, I blew it off too. Nowadays of course, my radar would've gone off and I'd have asked him, "Geoff, what's wrong? Are you sick? Do you need some help?" But how would a seven-year-old even know to ask that?

One day when I got home, my mom was just hanging up the phone. I couldn't tell you what it was, but the energy was different; she was preoccupied with something. I could tell she had been on the phone for quite some time. She was quiet and busy in thought. Her typical "How was your day?" was different.

I went out to play as usual until dusk, when I was called in for dinner. My brother, mother, and I frequently ate before my dad got home. Being self-employed and having to make ends meet didn't always afford Howie the luxury of eating dinner with his family every night.

"Boys, how was school today? What did you end up buying for lunch? Were you able to get out on the blacktop for recess because of the rain?" Mom was beating around the bush with superficial talk, and then—*Boom*—like a bomb, it hit. Her eyes welled up with tears, which made my eyes well up as well.

"There's something I have to tell you. You're not gonna like it."

What could be so wrong? Are we gonna have to go with her to the laundromat? I wondered.

She took a deep breath. "I spoke with Geoff's mom for quite a bit today. Geoff has been diagnosed with leukemia, and they don't know if he'll survive the treatment."

"What?" I asked. "What do you mean? What's leukemia?"

I started to cry because this was not what I'd been taught about the world. Kids didn't get sick. Kids didn't die. I ran to my room and covered my head with my favorite blanket and cried. *What if my best friend dies?*

Mom explained to me that all those appointments and doctors' visits were to confirm that he in fact had leukemia. In 1979, that was medical territory that hadn't been well researched; most children did not survive this disease. I'd heard of kids who had spent most of the rest of their lives in the hospital undergoing chemotherapy and all kinds of other drug therapies. The treatments were so dangerous and harsh that most people and particularly weak seven-year-olds couldn't tolerate the cure, and there were no GoFundMe pages to lighten the burden on families or social media sites to create meal trains or to raise awareness of such diseases let alone neighbors who had this awful disease.

I felt empty and very sad that night. I wondered how I was going to talk with Geoff in the morning. I waited for the school bus with my brother that next day. I was so nervous. Geoff didn't know I knew he was sick, and I didn't know what to say to my best friend who I thought was going to die. I didn't know how long it would take for the disease to steal his life. Would I lose him in days, or would it be a year?

When I got on the bus, there was no Geoff. After the pledge of allegiance and morning announcements, Mrs. Davis let the class know that Geoff was sick and would be out of school for a few weeks. Most of the kids didn't understand and went about their day patiently waiting for recess.

Two weeks went by quickly, and my mom gave me updates every couple of days after she had talked with Geoff's mom. He was very sick and had to stay in the hospital for the whole two weeks because his immune system was so weak from the treatments that he couldn't risk getting sick. A simple cold could possibly have taken his life. I missed him. I didn't have any close friends but him, so his absence was a large void in my first-grade school life. I hoped he would have a speedy recovery and be back to normal after those two weeks. Pure surrealism.

Geoff came back two weeks later after his treatment; he looked tired, pale, and thin, but he was his usual self. He came back to school all caught up; Mrs. Davis had given his mom his assignments to work on while he was in the hospital. He had his Red Sox hat on that day, and he was in good spirits. He told me that he was fatigued and didn't want to come back to class until he was able to stay the full day because he was nervous about what people would think about him and the way he looked.

It was a rainy, windy, and cold October day, which meant blacktop recess only—no playing in the grass and mud. We all filed outside to the small blacktop tucked behind the gymnasium; it had a few basketball hoops and hopscotch and four-square courts. We always have three to four teachers' aides who kept us out of trouble. When the whistle blew, it was time to line up quickly or else.

Geoff and I were chatting while getting ready to play some four square when a gust of wind blew Geoff's Red Sox hat off. It was as if the world stopped for a second; everyone was looking at poor Geoff as if he were an alien. He was completely bald; his scalp was as bright and pink as a newborn's. It looked very fragile and tender as if it had never seen light. He looked mortified, embarrassed. If there was a small hole in the blacktop that day, he would've shoved himself into it. Tears started rolling from his eyes down his cheeks as if to say how humiliated he was.

After I shook off my amazement and my eyes got back into their sockets, I ran for his hat, which was zooming around as if it were a balloon losing air. I finally snagged it and ran back to Geoff as if I were running for a touchdown, and I got it on his head. We were silent for a moment. We saw kids whispering and pointing and of course a few jackasses laughing and making fun of him.

"What happened to your hair? I didn't know what to do out there," I said when things quieted down.

"The medicine I'm taking for my leukemia makes me lose all my hair!" he said.

When he started to cry again, I felt uncomfortable. "Well, it doesn't matter to me," I said as I laughed nervously. "You wanna go bike riding after school? Either way, you're my best friend, and we'll stick together through this."

We never showed our emotions in my home let alone talk about them or cry in front of someone. I had no idea what was going to become of my best friend, but I knew he needed me to be a solid friend.

That day, I went home and had my mom take me to Rocco's barbershop in Scituate to have my hair shaved off. I was going to be just like Geoff. Everyone knew Rocco; he was the barber everyone went to. He had a bucket on a shelf full of Bazooka chewing gum, the kind with a cartoon on the wrapper. We always looked forward to getting a piece after our haircuts. It was great bubble- blowing gum.

I got on the bus that next day with my new whiffle haircut, nothing but stubble all the way around proud and sure. I sat with my friend Geoff with his Red Sox hat on and my whiffle haircut; we were two peas in a pod.

I spent most of the next few weeks sticking up for Geoff with the name-callers and bullies. Recess became a game for the mean kids to see who could steal Geoff's hat. I wasn't having it. I protected Geoff every day from those kids including getting into a few fist fights here and there. I wasn't afraid to fight off bullies; I spent most of grade school doing that for a lot of kids who were picked on. Lots of principal office and detention time, but it was worth it. Geoff went on to miraculously recover from leukemia, and we continued to be great friends through elementary school.

In junior high and high school, Geoff and I went our separate ways and hung out with different people, but we always had a special bond that no one would ever understand. I was always very grateful for his friendship and for our fun summers and school years together. We always said hello or gave the infamous subtle head nod in the hallway on our way to class.

These days, we have support groups and resources such as Buzz Off Cancer that help raise money for people with cancer. But back then, we didn't do that; I just wanted to show Geoff that I cared in the only way I knew how. I knew that Geoff knew that I had saved his life in first grade and that I was proud and honored to be his friend during that time. I'm really glad Geoff survived.

It was a beautiful day to help him save his own life.

My friend Geoff in remission

Chapter 5

Music, Tennis, and Camp with Eric

SECOND AND THIRD GRADES WEREN'T as much fun for me as first grade with Mrs. Davis had been. I spent most of second grade in trouble for talking during class and fighting bullies, and I spent third grade at a desk in a three-walled cubicle. Back then, most teachers and parents didn't know what to do for kids with extra energy. Nowadays, we call it ADHD, and there's a slew of treatments that work to help kids deal with their issues.

Mrs. Daneau, my third-grade teacher, thought it would be helpful to keep me after school every day. She was a short, stout woman with a wonderful ability to use her voice to calm down overenergized kids. I'd come out of my three-walled desk, head to the gymnasium, run around the gym a hundred and fifty times, and then she would drive me home. She lived just around the corner, and those days, people did things like that without any problem. I think that she thought if she fatigued my body, I would settle down. Ha! It just wound me up more of course.

In those days, we had a lot of freedom. Many days, I would get off the bus at a friend's house or walk home from school after playing in the schoolyard, so not getting home right after school wasn't always noticed and certainly not a thing. But Mom brought that to an abrupt halt when she heard that I was staying after school every day because I was so restless and inattentive. She sought the necessary help for me in the form of a therapist. I had some leftover anger due to my parents' divorce; I was too young to really understand why it had happened and why I had a new dad.

I spent the last few years of elementary school causing a little trouble here and there but primarily fighting bullies who picked on kids who couldn't defend themselves. I liked to fight, and I was pretty good at it for an overweight adolescent. I was wearing large sizes often labeled Husky back then, and I definitely had plenty of belly pudge with love handles. I was active but with a lot of weight. At junior high and high school, fighting was not tolerated. Plus, I was in all honors classes, so my time was filled with studying rather than fighting.

Howie's strong work ethic was evident in everything he did from running his own business to building a large addition on our house. He passed that ethic on to my brother and me. As soon as I could work legally, at age fifteen, I got a job. I had mowed lawns and babysat to make some money, but then I was able to earn a real paycheck at Quik Pik, the convenience store in Norwell. I'd get dropped off three days a week by the school bus and work afternoons, and I opened the doors at 6:00 a.m. on weekends and sold Sunday newspapers. The place was owned by a nice gentleman named Larry, who was always very respectful of me; I worked hard in return.

Summers in high school were always fun. I had taken a liking to music in elementary school, and I continued to chase music in junior high and high school. I played the clarinet and really enjoyed playing first chair in the high school band with another girl. She was really smart and very musical, so there was always some competition between us, which made us better.

I also loved to sing, and I played the piano. When I was a freshman, my parents asked me if I wanted to attend a music camp during the summer. I was unsure initially, but after reading the pamphlet (long before the internet), I decided to attend for two weeks.

The camp offered activities such as swimming and tennis in addition to workshops on music. Going turned out to be a great decision; I attended the camp during the following two summers. I stayed the entire eight weeks it was open because I'd met wonderful people with the same interest I had in music.

Arthur and Ellen Booth had started the Northeast Music Camp in the early seventies in Ware, Massachusetts. Of course the running joke for people when you told them it was in Ware was "Where?" Ha ha ha. Ware is in the middle of the Berkshires in western Massachusetts, where the landscape is beautiful; it's brimming with woods and lots of nice bodies of water. It's home to the Quabbin Reservoir, the largest inland body of water in Massachusetts and Boston's primary water supply. Bald eagles soar overhead, and I sometimes had the pleasure of seeing some whitetail deer or a cute black bear. It was a peaceful place to be; throughout the grounds, I heard all kinds of instruments in the practice cabins or happy voices playing games in the fields.

The grounds were massive; we walked everywhere. We had baseball and softball diamonds and four square, tetherball, tennis, and volleyball courts. We campers lived in cabins based on our ages, and smack dab in the middle of the cabins lived Don and Donna (Ma) Kitson. They ran a tight ship but were full of love, and we respected them. A tall flagpole with a bell was in front of their cabin. Every morning and evening, a flag ceremony was held, and one of our trumpet players played as the flag was raised and lowered and folded.

Our camp was on Hardwick Pond, which had a beach and two boathouses. We had Friday night sing-alongs and campfires at the beach and water competitions and carnivals on the weekends. I earned my lifeguard certification the last summer I was there. It took me the entire eight weeks, and the test was by no means easy. We participated in arts and crafts, archery, canoeing, and a million other field games. Every two weeks, a large concert was held to showcase the talents of the concert band, chorus, treble choir, orchestra, and jazz band. It was a great camp that offered the perfect blend of disciplined musical programming and extracurriculars. Many of the friends I made there went on to become professional musicians, and many of us today still play for fun with friends or our children.

In 1986, Mr. Booth passed away after a long health issue. At the end of the 1989 season, the camp closed. That last season was quite a year for me. I was going to be a senior in high school and was turning seventeen in August.

I made a lot of close friends at camp, and one of my closest friends was Eric. He was from a suburb in Massachusetts; we connected on day one when we met in the Ellington cabin. He was a gentle young man. He wore a sling on his left arm, which was clearly smaller than his right arm, and his left shoulder and left side of his face and chin looked abnormal. He wore a plastic foot brace in his sneaker and walked with an odd gait. Knowing what I know now about medical conditions, I assume he had had a stroke as an infant and had lost use of his left side. But with bracing and some therapy, he was functioning pretty well.

He was an amazing French horn player; he would pull his left arm and hand out of his sling and shove his hand in the horn while he played—pretty normal position for a French horn player, right? Eric could make the most beautiful, full, warm sounds and tones with his horn, and I loved listening to him practice. I still love the warmness of the French horn, and whenever I see an orchestra and hear that familiar sound, I think of Eric and my summers at Northeast Music Camp.

Eric and I never discussed his physical disability; I think we were too young and probably too uncomfortable to be that transparent with each other, but we enjoyed each other's company, and we loved music.

We enjoyed playing tennis; despite his disability and the use of only one really strong right arm and one really fast foot, Eric could cover his whole side of the court. I lost game after game to him. He had a topspin on his forehand and a mean right backhand. He could play the short game and the long game equally well. He knew it was one thing he was really good at except of course the French horn, and he was proud and a little showy at times. He would nicely joke and laugh at me while I chased his balls to the corners and to the net and back again huffing and puffing away unable to keep up. He had some droop on the left side of his face that made his smile unforgettable, contagious, and goofy.

One Saturday morning in August, the sun was bright and hot, and the sky was the color of a bluebird. We had free time to do whatever we wanted on Saturday mornings because we always performed a concert for the parents picking up their sons and daughters whose sessions were ending. It was game on that day. Eric and I had talked the night before about playing tennis, and I had confidently done some trash talking about beating him in tennis because I said that his game was starting to slip. Funny, right?

The tennis courts were on the other side of the field tucked in among giant pine trees that offered a hair of shade from the relentless sun. It was in the high eighties, but in the direct sun on a paved tennis court, it felt like a hundred and ten. Eric and I walked across the field and pulled our tennis racquets out of our fancy Dunlop racquet bags. We showed up every year with something new and fancy to mark our territory and show how serious we were about our tennis game.

"You serve first, Eric, and don't drop the ball!" I said laughing.

"OK, smart-ass! Get ready to get smoked like a cheap cigar!"

That was the way it went; two kids thinking they were Andre Agassi and John McEnroe playing at Wimbledon. Attitude, sarcasm, and a lot of bullshit slinging. I was hell-bent on winning that game. We went back and forth a few times each scoring a few volleys. Sweat starting to roll down our foreheads, and our faces were flushed. I had to back up my mouth and try to get a win. For a change, it was a tie for the set. Next point would win the set. Eric served a fast one down the line, and I tried my all to get to that ball and *Pop!* I returned it! Fast serves often ended up going out of bounds, but that time, it landed on the line. Eric had to find a way to return it, and he did, but it hit the white of the net and dropped back on his side. "Come on!" Eric shouted.

"One set for Team Miller!" I danced to the front of the net to grab a ball.

Eric walked up to the net. I waited for what I thought would be a boastful comment, but he looked at eye to eye and said, "Go away! Get away from me! Go away." He waved his good arm at me. We were almost face to face. I was confused. In a few seconds, Eric's face went grey. He started spinning on his feet, and *Boom!* He fell face first and sideways onto the scorching hot court pavement. . His body was shaking uncontrollably. He sounded like he was choking. I freaked out. I was alone. I knew something terrible was wrong. I looked all around, but no one was in sight.

I ran as fast as I could around to his side of the net and rolled him over. "Eric! Eric! *Fuck!* What's wrong? Eric? What's the matter? Can you hear me?"

Eric was still making choking noises, and his arms and legs were flailing uncontrollably. I saw a giant wet spot on the front of his shorts and knew he had urinated. His pupils were rolled in the back of his head, and his face was lifeless, flat. I thought he was dying. I had zero medical experience and didn't know what was wrong with him. We had never talked about his disability because it had never defined him. I had never seen this happen to him or anyone else. This went on for a few minutes; I hoped that it would just stop or that I would just wake up from this nightmare. Neither happened.

The infirmary was several hundred yards away straight up a paved walkway. I had no choice. There was no one around to ask for help I picked Eric up and carried him like a bundle of wood. I ran as fast as my overweight, out of shape body would let me. Eric was still unresponsive and convulsing as we moved, which made carrying him even more difficult.

I was so out of breath. I was struggling. I had to get him to the infirmary. Something was desperately wrong with my favorite tennis partner and my favorite French horn player. I had to save him. There was nothing left in my tank when I reached the crest of the hill wheezing and out of breath. My biceps were cramped. I started down to the infirmary.

The nurse came flying out of her office to meet me. Someone had seen me carrying a lifeless body up the hill and had reported it to Ma Kitson at the main cabin, and she must have then called the nurse. We had only rotary dial phones then, and boy were they slow to dial when you were in an emergency. It was like your fingers wouldn't work and you kept missing the right numbered hole.

I was exhausted as I dropped Eric on the gurney. My arms were stuck bent. I could barely catch my breath. I fell to my knees looking right into his soul. "Please, God! Help him! I beg you!"

Eric was unconscious and unresponsive. The nurse had one of the counselors rush me out of the infirmary so she could do her assessment. I heard sirens coming down that quiet road in Ware that was rarely traveled except by parents to drop off and pick up campers.

Everything seemed to be in slow motion as I thumped down the steps of the infirmary gasping … I could hear and feel my rapid breath resonating throughout my body and the pounding of each of my footsteps down the stairs. Loud. Echoing internally. My heartbeat was thudding … Sirens in the background … People talking to me in what seemed to be slow, slurred speech. What the hell had just happened? I returned to my cabin and lay on my bunk just staring at the springs of the mattress above me. I replayed that tennis game over and over wondering what had happened.

I later found out that Eric had epilepsy. I didn't know what that meant. The nurse visited me later that afternoon to check on me; she knew that I had been traumatized.

"Brett, Eric had a prolonged grand mal seizure. He could have died had you not been there with him and not taken action." She gazed at me solemnly.

"I didn't know what to do, but I knew I had to do something fast. I was so scared. I never saw anyone's body do that before."

"If you had let it take its course and not sought help, he might not have been so lucky. He could have choked to death or suffered an injury to an already fragile brain."

I was on the verge of tears.

Eric came back to camp late Sunday night, and he was so grateful when he saw me. He came over to my bunk still fatigued from the event and said, "Thanks for your help. I'm so glad you were there." He was weepy and still a little embarrassed, but he had retained his sense of humor. "You owe me a rematch, smart-ass."

We were young, and it was hard for us to express ourselves emotionally, but Eric cried many a time that summer when we were alone and thanked me for saving his life. He didn't remember anything about the incident or what had led up to it, and I was glad about that; no one should have to remember such bodily trauma, and no one should ever have to go through the embarrassment of a situation like that. Eric was told what had happened by a few people who knew the story, and he would always be grateful.

Two kids playing tennis, playing music, and living their best lives as friends. That Saturday in August at Northeast Music Camp was a beautiful day to save a life.

Eric at Northeast Music Camp

Chapter 6

The Finger of Fate

SENIOR YEAR AT NORWELL HIGH couldn't come quickly enough for me. I didn't care much for high school, and I had many detentions and a few too many suspensions under my belt mostly for insubordination and a few pranks I played on my not-so-favorite AP teachers. I didn't like to eat lunch from 10:50 to 11:15, and I didn't understand why at age sixteen I had to raise my hand and ask to go to the bathroom.

Also, I didn't play any sports. Instead, I chose to work, which is what we were taught in my family, and that served me well later in life. I continued to take the bus to work after school every day and cleaned and stocked shelves at the Quik Pik. On Sundays, I would get there early and make up all the Sunday *Boston Globe* papers. All the coupons and ads as well as the sections that weren't time sensitive came on Saturdays, and I had to put the cover stories and news that was printed on Saturday nights into the other two sections. I also sold the fresh donuts that were delivered early that morning as well. It was a great job, and I worked there all my high school years.

I was in all advanced placement classes except math, which I just couldn't understand well. I was always in class with the "wicked smaht" kids, which was bizarre because I liked to cause mischief but always out of fun and I think for attention as well.

It was my first semester of my senior year in 1989, and I knew I had to buckle down second semester, the semester colleges focus on, the big one that weighed heavily on whether they would accept you.

Despite my goofing off, I was seventeenth in my class of 148, which was OK, but unfortunately, I did poorly on my SATs. My guidance counselor didn't really give me any guidance except for telling me I needed to apply to more safety schools because I didn't have a shot at the University of Connecticut or Northeastern. I think he just thought I was a troublemaker with the rap sheet I had created and wasn't serious about college. I ignored his recommendation and just hoped I'd be accepted by one of the schools I'd applied to.

And Northeastern it would be! I was accepted into the Bouvé College of Health Sciences, a very well-known school in NU that had multiple health care curricula depending on what you wanted to study. I decided to go there and pick a major there later when I was sure what I wanted to do.

The problem of paying for NU came up; how were we going to come up with the $13,000, which did not include books and other expenses? I couldn't live there not only because of the cost of room and board but also because I needed to work. But I wasn't afraid of that; I worked multiple jobs while studying.

I had a backup plan, though, and it was an exciting backup plan.

My grandfather, father, and brother had served in the military in prestigious divisions with outstanding people, and I decided to do the same. I enlisted in the US Army to be a combat medic—Surprise! After multiple meetings with my army recruiter and a review of my scores on my Armed Services Vocational Aptitude Battery test, all results pointed me in the direction of combat medicine. I was slated to leave for boot camp at Fort Dix, New Jersey, four days after I graduated high school, on May 28, 1990, and that's what I did. I would then be able to qualify for the GI Bill, which would be enough money to help with my commuting expenses and some of my books. My master plan was laid out.

I graduated high school in May 1990 and was finally free to live my life somewhat the way I wanted. I said goodbye to a few friends I had and started to mentally prepare for my departure with Uncle Sam. I was excited to embark on a new adventure but equally as nervous as you can imagine.

The military was the best thing that ever happened to me. The discipline, attention to detail, and the strong self-esteem built by my drill sergeants created an attitude of second to none and an esprit de corps with zero tolerance for quitting. I finally had a strong purpose and an unstoppable mental drive.

When I graduated on that field at Fort Dix in the summer of 1990 with hundreds of other soldiers, I was eighteen, mentally and physically fit, proud, and the sharpest I'd ever been. It was the beginning of the rest of my life; I could be anything I wanted to be and accomplish anything I was willing to work for. Keep running towards your dreams they said.

I had left high school in Massachusetts at 230 pudgy pounds and left New Jersey twelve weeks later a 168-pound machine. I was unrecognizable to my family and friends when I came home on leave. My muscles were shredded, my posture was one of confidence, and my mental state was focused and self-aware. I was running three to ten miles daily, eating a strict, healthy diet, and staying mentally and spiritually fit. It was the start of a completely new chapter in life.

I graduated combat medic school at the top of my class at Fort Sam Houston in San Antonio, Texas, and passed my emergency medical technician (EMT) licensing exam. To qualify as an army combat medic, a soldier must go through an additional sixteen weeks of advanced medical training. The priority and duty of a combat medic is to treat soldiers who are casualties of enemy fire. Their knowledge and skills require them to manage combat casualties from the point of injury right through to the evacuation phase.

The duties of a combat medic include caring for acute trauma such as airway management, stabilizing broken bones, administering medication, and inserting intravenous fluids or subcutaneous injections. The training, skills and job correlate most closely in the civilian world to those of a paramedic on an ambulance. Paramedics are authorized to give treatments and injections and perform certain procedures in the field. In contrast, an EMT has a more restricted set of techniques and options. The basic difference between EMTs and paramedics lies in their level of education and kind of procedures they are allowed to perform well. EMTs can administer CPR, glucose, and oxygen while paramedics can perform more-complex procedures such as inserting

IV lines, administering drugs, and applying external defibrillators for cardiac rhythm changes.

During training, combat medics acquire a working knowledge of dentistry, optometry, veterinary care, preventative medicine, and water sanitation to better serve their teammates who may be foreign counterparts where health care facilities are nonexistent. What seems initially to be unnecessary training ultimately became my most important training. Most army combat medics earn the nickname "Doc" when they're assigned to their duty stations. They are highly respected among their peers for obvious reasons—They keep people alive.

I decided to pursue physical therapy as a major at Northeastern in Boston. I wanted more, demanded more, and expected more from myself all the time.

Funny enough, after I finished my initial training for the army and enlisted in the army Reserves, I landed back at the Quik Pik working nights on the register. That was very helpful because I could study in between customers.

Physical therapy school was extremely demanding. I also continued to do landscaping and plow snow in the winter for extra income. It was a struggle paying for college, but between my multiple jobs including a coop program at school, which was a paid job, the GI Bill, and my folks, we made it work.

After my weight loss and change into a physically fit person, one of the most important things for me was to maintain my mental, physical, and spiritual fitness. I exercised every day; I ran and did one to two hours of weight training at a gym in Hanover, the next town over. It was a well cared for and clean fitness facility whose members were often people my age. They had a great weight room, a steam room, a pool, a basketball court, and racquetball courts. It was a cool place to hang, and I spent one to two hours there every day if I could. I became very friendly with the staff and many fellow weight lifters and racquetball competitors. If I had to work late, I would drive to Boston early and go to the school's gym, which opened at 5:00 a.m. Oh to be young and full of energy!

Those early mornings were tough especially with school, commuting in Boston's constant traffic (this was before the Big Dig project), and possibly having to work the next night as well.

One beautiful day in February 1992, the sunset was one of those gorgeous, pink-orange winter skies. I headed to the gym to get some weightlifting in and some pool work. I had decided to venture into sprint triathlon competitions, so I had added swimming to my regime. It was a typical afternoon with a lot of folks coming in after work, but as the evening went on, a lot of folks came in after dinner and the crowd shifted a little, but it was always a large mix and great energy. I'd see familiar faces and strike up conversations between sets.

I finished my weight training that night and always did my swim training afterward because it felt so nice on my worked muscles. I had just finished the bent-over Nautilus row machine and headed for the locker room. As I turned to the locker room entrance, I heard a terrifying, high-pitched scream, one that could never be mistaken for anything other than very bad news. The high pitch of this scream rocked the walls and eardrums of every member there People were racing away from the center of the weight room. I spun around and saw a man. I could tell by the look on his face that the screaming was coming from his three-year-old daughter, who was jumping up and down while emitting a terrible, high-pitched tone that sent adults into spasms of fear and concern.

"What's the matter?" her father asked her frantically.

There was blood everywhere; that made it hard to tell what was going on. I ran into the situation as others, screaming, ran the other way. It was so confusing and pure mayhem.

It was at this point that I realized what had happened to this poor little girl. Somehow, Michelle, the girl, had walked into the weight room while her dad was exercising on the Nautilus chest press and stuck her finger in the weight rack; she had severed it. She was jumping up and down shaking her hand screaming; there was her finger stuck under 150 pounds of steel plates.

"Lift the weights up!" I demanded. "I need to get her finger out of the machine. It's severed. It's under the plates." I grabbed the bloody finger carefully so I wouldn't disturb the tissue any further. It was a timing issue; her finger had not been dislocated, but the tissue was torn and discolored.

I scooped up the finger and Michelle and handed her to her dad. "Let's go!" I ordered.

It was like the Red Sea parting as I ran to the front desk to grab what supplies I needed. People scattered at the sight of something that most had never seen—lots of blood. I saw empathy on every parent's face and fear on every other face. As frequently happens in such situations, everything seemed to be in slow motion though things were actually hectic and moving very fast.

I saw horror on the receptionist's face as I approached her and held up the finger. I said, "Call the ambulance, and get me a first aid kit and a Ziploc bag with a little bit of water and some ice. I'm going to the front door to meet the paramedics. Hurry!"

We didn't have 911 systems in place back then; we just called fire and police departments directly. I rummaged through the first aid kit and found lots of band aids, a roll of gauze, and some tape. I grabbed the bag with the ice and water and ran upstairs with Michelle and her dad to the lobby area, where it was quiet and I could work. I put the finger in the bag of ice and water and sealed it. I handed it to her father and said, "Dad, hang onto this. Everything's going to be fine. My name is Brett by the way."

"Frank." He nodded hands shaking.

He had no idea that this muscular college kid was an army combat medic with an EMT license, but I could tell he knew I was sure of myself and my skills. I applied the gauze and taped up Michelle's hand. She was small; though the finger had been severed below the nail, it was pretty much her whole finger, which made applying pressure to such a funky shape difficult. I tried my best to console her, but of course she continued to cry out in pain and fear.

My hands were shaking from just leaving the weight room; my muscles were fatigued. She was in her dad's arms sitting on his lap on the floor. He had called his wife on the front desk's cordless phone and was trying to explain what had happened over Michelle's crying. You could imagine the guilt he felt.

We sat in the corner of the lobby for about fifteen minutes, which seemed like fifteen hours, waiting for the ambulance. When it arrived, we rushed out the door. "Hand the finger over," I said to Frank. I gave the EMT the goods. "This is a three-year-old female, no past medical history, and her dad. Her finger was severed in a weight machine about fifteen, twenty minutes ago. The finger's on ice, and the bleeding is controlled on the hand. Please don't stop at the community hospital. She needs to go to Children's Hospital right away for the best possible outcome. I'm an army combat medic and licensed EMT. I did you right."

Her hand and finger needed a pediatric hand surgery specialist and a plastic surgeon. Frank thanked me and climbed into the ambulance. He was naturally distracted by all the commotion and the worrisome thoughts of whether she would be able to use her hand again with all its fingers.

I went to the locker room to wash the blood off my hands, change my bloodstained workout clothes, and get my gear. People looked at me as if I'd just come back from war, but the army had trained me well, and I thrived on helping people in situations that no one else could or wanted to.

I left that night for home to do some school work and didn't find out until later what happened with Michelle. The following weekend, Tim, the fitness facility manager, offered me a position as a personal trainer, and I worked there for a couple of years to continue to contribute to my college tuition. I met a lot of wonderful people there and learned a lot about the fitness industry.

About two weeks after the severed finger event, I got a phone call. "In the second between hello and how are you, I immediately recognized the voice and hoped that this had a happy ending. Brett, Frank Granara here. I called to say thank you. The surgeon was able to reattach Michelle's finger with a bovine skin graft, and she should have full functionality of her hand after some rehab. The doctor told me that the actions you took that night saved her finger's ability to be reattached and that because of it, full function was guaranteed. I don't know what to say but thank you very much."

"I was happy to be able to help," I said.

I was elated to hear the news, and in my typical fashion, I disregarded all the compliments from the family and carried on about my evening.

That day at the fitness center was a beautiful day to save lives. And fingers.

Alert EMT saves finger

With all the depressing news printed, we would like to inform you and your readers of the help we have received when my daughter had an accident.

My 3-year-old daughter, Michelle, who was with me at a gym on Feb. 8, put her finger in a weight machine and the pulley severed her finger just below the nail.

A young man named Brett Miller of Norwell, an EMT who was working out at the gym, came to our aid. He was instinctive enough to retrieve the finger, put it on ice and help me treat my daughter's wound.

We took Michelle to Children's Hospital in Boston where doctors and nurses told us he had done a great job in his treatment.

After several hours the doctor successfully reattached her finger and in several subsequent visits the hand specialists tell us that there should be full use of the finger with no long-term adverse effects.

This story has a happy ending because of the efforts of Mr. Brett Miller. We thank him.

FRANK, JEAN
& MICHELLE GRANARA
Norwell

An article from the *Patriot Ledger*

February 21, 1992

Mr. William B. Ketter
Patriot Ledger
Editorial Dept.
400 Crown Colony Drive
Quincy, MA 02169

Dear Mr. Ketter,

With all the depressing new printed, we would like to inform
you and your readers of the help we have received when my
daughter had an accident.

I had my 3 year old daughter Michelle with me at a gym on
Saturday, February 8th. She managed to put her finger in a
weight machine and the pulley severed her finger just below
the nail.

In the confusion, a young man named Brett Miller of Norwell
came to our aid. Mr. Miller is an EMT who was working out
at the gym. He was instinctive enough to retrieve the
finger from the machine, put it on ice and then help me
treat my daughters wound.

After he immobilized the wound, we took Michelle to
Childrens Hospital in Boston. The doctors and nurses told
us that he had done a great job in his treatment. After
several hours the doctor successfully reattached her finger.

In several subsequent visits to the hospital, the hand
specialists tell us that there should be full use of the
finger with no long term adverse effects.

This story has a happy ending because of the efforts of Mr.
Brett Miller. We thank him.

Sincerely,

Frank, Jean and Michelle Granara

A letter from Michelle's family to the editor of the *Patriot Ledger*

45

Chapter 7

Highway to Hell: Bosnia

I CONTINUED TO TRAIN AS AN army combat medic and attend college at the same time; I was on the fast track to becoming a physical therapist. There was also the possibility of continuing schooling after graduation to challenge the entry-level exams to become a physician. This was a dual-time program; I could go to school and serve at the same time using the GI bill to pay for my education. It was a terrific win–win for me and the army.

I had completed boot camp in September 1990 at Fort Dix and graduated in the top of my class in regard to my combat medic training in San Antonio, Texas. I served two years on active duty and I was flushed into the US Army Reserves for the next six years. That commitment meant a weekly meeting in Boston with my teammates, one full weekend every month, and two weeks in the summer. On what we called reserve weekends, I'd be up at Fort Devens in Ayer, Massachusetts, working as the lead noncommissioned officer (NCO) on deployment, construction, and breakdown of the mobile hospital system that was newly introduced by the government known as DEPMEDS, deployable medical systems. I was attached to a combat support hospital similar to a MASH-style unit; we needed to be able to go anywhere at any time to provide medical support in any setting in the world.

Other reserve weekend deployments meant participating in practice mass-casualty events where there would be civilian or military disasters. As a unit, we would need to triage, treat, and evacuate injured people. I had taken the time also to be certified as a range NCOIC (noncommissioned officer in charge) for range safety, and the qualifying and shooting of the 9 mm pistol. I spent multiple weekends qualifying our military personnel who required a yearly pistol-firing event. This would later turn out to be very valuable to me.

I was surprised to be issued orders in April 1996 to be deployed under the United States European Command to lead in the effort of establishing the Joint Contact Team Program, which included members of the special operations primarily because of their language skills and active component personnel as well. The mission of this partnership program was to link the United States with designated partner countries through NATO to support the security cooperation objectives and create new self-defense forces.

I was chosen to assist the Macedonian government and military treat the thousands maimed by land mines in Bosnia by setting up their hospital systems to deal with the issue. Far from modern facilities, these treatment centers were crude and dirty compared to US medicine protocols.

Some history here. Civil war in Bosnia-Herzegovina erupted in April 1992. Over the next three and a half years, between 140,000 and 250,000 people were killed. Ninety percent of these deaths were noncombatants … Ninety percent.

An unknown number of people had been wounded or maimed by the land mines that saturated the country. As many as 12,000 women were raped, and 520,000 Bosnians found themselves homeless and fleeing their once beautiful and family-oriented neighborhoods. A large number of diplomatic initiatives and potential truces failed before a US agreement in late 1995—the Dayton Peace Accords—finally ended the fighting and permitted US military forces to enter the country as part of the NATO international force.

Unfortunately, the UN failed to protect the safe area of Srebrenica in July 1995, and the Srebrenica massacre occurred. At least 8,000 mostly Muslim men and boys were chased through woods in and around Srebrenica by Serbian troops in what is considered the worst carnage of civilians in Europe since World War II. This slaughter has been confirmed as an act of genocide.

In addition to the killings, more than 20,000 civilians were expelled from the area in a process known as ethnic cleansing; that created over 1.3 million refugees, many of whom had fled to other countries including Germany, Austria, Sweden, the Netherlands, and Denmark, desperately trying to escape the fighting that engulfed the region.

The massacre, the worst episode of mass murder, left deep emotional scars on survivors and created enduring obstacles to political reconciliation among Bosnia's ethnic groups. It required years of scientific analysis using laborious comparisons of soil and tissue samples, shell casings, pollen, and clothing fragments to piece together exactly where the killings had occurred and how the bodies had been moved among an estimated eighty mass grave sites. By early 2010, the International Commission on Missing Persons, a nongovernmental organization established in 1996, had used DNA samples to identify more than 6,400 individual victims.

It was originally estimated that at least 200,000 people were killed and more than 2,000,000 displaced during the 1992–95 war.

In this grim situation, I entered the small hospital in Skopje, Macedonia, in what looked like the middle of hell on April 14, 1996. I saw tattered children in the quiet streets. The young and very young were all alone, playing games that looked familiar to those I played in my childhood. They seemed happy hanging out, playing marbles with pebbles, kicking cans down a dirt alley, and throwing sticks to one another. There were no Big Wheels, Ping-Pong tables, or TVs to entertain them; all they had was dirt and rocks to play with. They were unkempt and wearing whatever was available like homeless people in the United States. I thought this couldn't be. It smelled like it had just rained, creating a moldy and musky scent. Wild dogs roamed the streets barking as if looking for homes too.

In contrast to the seemingly carefree children, entire families huddled together outside the hospital entrance. Many looked homeless. Many looked afraid. The city looked like it had not been updated in a hundred years. Macedonia was dreary, cloudy, and rainy. It was depressing and hopeless. During my tour of the archaic facility that they called a hospital, I saw many refugee casualties and men, women, and children who had been maimed by land mines that had not been recovered. It was an ongoing problem despite the war being over.

Bosnian hospitals were overcrowded, undersupplied, understaffed, and completely unable to provide basic health care for residents much less provide prosthetics for the thousands who had been mutilated by land mines.

Refugees had been shuffled and evacuated all over the place with and without their families. Families that had lost loved ones or who had been separated were packed in rooms. They were homeless, dirty, and wearing torn clothes. They looked as if they hadn't bathed recently. The hospital smelled like a cross between body odor and mercurochrome. Babies were crying constantly. Children were on the cement floors somehow sleeping through all the noise; they were probably allowing their bodies to finally rest after being in such fear for so long. They must have felt that it was OK to close their eyes and hope for some new form of stability. These families didn't have the luxury of bribing doctors to care for them—another big issue for the Bosnian health care system.

Wherever I walked, all eyes were on me, an American. I looked different from any other person they had seen, and it was obvious that I was from the United States. Posturally erect, muscular, clean cut, and stoic. Some gazed at me with their hollow eyes but many looked at me with curiosity and with a glimmer of hope. People were still hoping and praying for a better life for themselves and their children.

At the shabby hospital, parents and children wandered the halls, many aimlessly. Some searched for family members who may have been evacuated and brought to the facility. Nurses and doctors were tired but relentlessly working as nurses, doctors, personal care aides, respiratory therapists, physical therapists, and every other health care discipline all at the same time. People moaned, babies cried, and some patients were being whisked off to less than adequate surgical rooms. Mass confusion and not a lot of direction. I had no idea that this was what postwar Macedonia looked like and that the region was still in turmoil with great ethnic conflict.

I was there to make the situation better in conjunction with other international forces involved. We owed it to these people, who had suffered and endured injuries—some catastrophic—loss of life, loss of family, and relocation. All things I could never imagine.

After this eye-opening tour and a brief discussion with the central command of the Macedonian army, I stepped outside to process what I had seen and heard. The crying and moaning I had heard was replaced by the miraculous sound of kids laughing—a joyous sound. I saw a circle of kids playing marbles in the dirt, and I decided to engage them.

I walked to them slowly so as to not frighten them, and I sat on that dirt road like a six-year-old poor kid who had grown up at King's Landing in Norwell, Massachusetts. With no judgment and no cares, I played marbles with my new friends, who showed me unconditional love. Many of the very young kids stood away from me and just stared while others pointed at me and tapped me and ran off in a flirtatious way. Some sat in my lap or on my shoulders and enjoyed the stranger's attention. The older kids explained in broken English that they all were refugees from the war who had been separated from their families and were homeless vagabonds. They stuck together, and the older kids took care of the younger kids.

What in the hell had happened? What in the hell had these kids seen and endured in the last five years of massacre and ethnic cleansing? Looking deep into these kids' eyes, I saw unrest, hopelessness, and fear for the future. But as resilient kids, in the moment, they were happy. They were the most beautiful group of kids. I still see their sweet, innocent smiles. It took all of me and all that I represented to walk away from that game of marbles. They chased me all the way back to the hospital running around me and playing a touch-and-go teasing game. It made me remember that with great power came great responsibility and that I needed to do my part if for nothing else but for that group of homeless kids who invited this total stranger, no questions asked, to a game of marbles in the middle of a war zone.

It was a beautiful day to save lives.

Playing marbles on the streets of Bosnia with refugee children

Evacuees from the besieged Muslim enclave of Srebrenica
packed in a truck en route to Tuzla pass through Tojsici
on March 29, 1993 (AP Photo/Michel Euler)

Refugees from Srebrenica who had spent the night
in the open air gather outside the UN base at Tuzla
airport, July 14, 1995 (AP Photo/Darko Bandic)

Chapter 8

Highway to Hell:
A Mother's Nightmare

FROM 1990 THROUGH 1992, AFTER leaving active duty and while serving in the reserves, I remained disciplined in my physical and mental fitness world while being diligent in school. I thrived on the fascinating things that made the human body work, and I spent extra lab time dissecting cadavers for classmates. I really enjoyed the detail of the human body and what made it tick physically and mentally.

I landed a job just before graduation at a hospital in Plymouth, Massachusetts, the landmark of Plymouth Rock and the Pilgrims. Tons of history in a beautiful South Shore waterfront town. A colonel I knew was the director of rehabilitation in the Rehabilitation Services Department at the time; we had a mutual respect for each other's military service. It was a good fit employment-wise. I was to start that fall after graduating in September 1995. I was tied up in military training that summer, so it worked out quite well for our schedules.

I commuted from my family's home in Norwell for about a year until I could rent an apartment. In late 1997, I found a beautiful place on Priscilla Beach, a private beach in Manomet, a suburb of Plymouth. It connected to Whitehorse Beach, the public beach. It was a quaint town with a summer buzz, penny-candy stores, and locally owned restaurants. It was perfect, and my landlord was a gem.

Mr. Fantasia was an older, overweight gentleman disabled by chronic back pain. I think he had some ties to the mafia. He had multiple rentals in the area, but mine was in the perfect location. My apartment was under a house, and it had a separate entrance and a trail out my front door directly to the beach.

The Fantasias and I hit it off; I moved in in late summer and caught a few beautiful sunsets at the beach before the cold weather came. I spent my early mornings treating patients at the hospital and the rest of my days and nights exercising and running the beach. It was a beautiful time to be alive, and I took advantage of it.

The late nineties was a boom time for much of America, and the feeling of potential showed everywhere. From the TV shows to the movies, the sense of "Pull yourself up by your bootstraps" and rampant capitalism permeated our culture and the world. The Soviet Union was shattered, the Cold War was over, and Americans wanted to entertain themselves, buy these newfangled home computers, send emails, and spend money. McDonald's was super-sizing everything, and Furbies were at the top of every kid's Christmas list. O. J. Simpson was charged with murder, Harry Potter was released, Nancy Kerrigan was attacked, and JonBenet Ramsey disappeared. Google was launched, and Microsoft saved Apple from bankruptcy. It was a time when the media was changing from news and facts to sensationalism and chasing ratings. It was quite a change from my quiet seventies' upbringing.

When winter settled in, I found myself driving to Loon Mountain in Lincoln, New Hampshire, every Friday night to volunteer at a wonderful program I had found through my junior high school principal. White Mountain Adaptive Ski School had about twenty volunteers who sat in the heavy Boston traffic every Friday night to teach kids of all disabilities how to ski. This was before the Big Dig, the largest and most challenging highway project in the history of the United States with the goal of reducing traffic and improved mobility in one of America's oldest, most congested major cities. We had all kinds of disabled clients – deaf, blind, amputees, cerebral palsy, para- and quadriplegics, and rare diseases. We never refused anyone and we had a reputation for being an outstanding program with the most knowledgeable instructors. We would soon become the best program on the East Coast, and in time, we expanded our programming beyond skiing. By the time I finished volunteering at this program, I had spent eighteen years volunteering almost every weekend of every winter season. It was worth it.

At the hospital, as my experience as a licensed physical therapist increased, I started to become confident and to work more closely with the doctors and surgeons. I started to write new and improved protocols—established papers with procedures to follow for specific surgical interventions for total knee and hip replacements, ACL repairs, and post-mastectomy lymphedema protocols secondary to breast cancer.

I took advantage of my education benefits and pursued different certifications including becoming a certified lymphedema drainage therapist, and I became more specialized in joint mobilization and manipulation. I wanted to better myself and my PT skills so I could be more available to more people in need of help. I felt on the top of my therapy game, and my colleagues respected me. I saw more patients daily than any of my colleagues did, and I had a passion for my occupation and a gift of healing people who crossed my path.

Speaking of crossing paths, I met a beautiful, smart, young woman, also a physical therapist, and we enjoyed talking about our profession and the cutting-edge treatments that were coming along. Tina was recently divorced and had a two-year-old, so things between us started very slowly, but in a few months, we started a serious relationship and spent a lot of time together.

We were very careful about my involvement with her child for obvious reasons. I often visited her for a quick dinner or when her daughter was spending the weekend with her dad. Tina and I always enjoyed doing things together outside and spending time talking about quantum physics and the universe. She was always very complimentary about my being the best therapist at the hospital; she felt that I had received a special gift through the power of my hands. She often reminded me to use what I had because it had been given to me for a reason. And that's what I did.

Sunday nights were a time to wind down and get ready for the work week. Most every Sunday, I would drive the thirty minutes from Plymouth to Norwell and visit my parents. I'd help them with yardwork and other chores. It was always comforting for me to go home since it was where I had grown up and made many fond memories.

One particular Sunday wasn't any different. It was a lovely day; the sun was bright, and the air was warm for the fall. I had mowed the grass and raked leaves at my parents' house. I spent some time splitting wood for the winter for their wood stove, and then off I went back to Plymouth. When I got home, I had a beer and some food and took a hot shower. I set up all my clothes and things I would need for the work week arranged in order day by day. I had become very detailed and very organized in the military, and I enjoyed being squared away.

It was just about dusk, but I had a little extra light to enjoy wrapping up the weekend. After making sure I was good to go for the week, I decided to head over to Tina's house. It was a quick twenty-minute ride and two highway exits to get there. Off I went and onto Route 3 north; I merged with some of the Cape Cod tourists who were on their way home after their beach weekends. I was working my way toward the old Route 44 exit along the pet cemetery if you've ever traveled that way, so I was in the right lane.

I noticed a broken-down car in the far-left passing lane and a woman sitting in the car looking pretty frightened. Due to all the usual Cape Cod traffic and the unerring propensity of Massachusetts drivers to tailgate their opponents at eighty mph, cars were flying by barely dodging the woman's car. Because of the lack of distance between cars, most drivers could not react until they were on top of this disabled vehicle.

This was a recipe for a terrible disaster; this poor woman was frozen in fear and didn't know what to do. I pulled over on the right-hand side of the road. These were the mid- to late nineties, the days of flip phones with mediocre reception, and 911 services were not established in every town as they are today. I called Tina, told her where I was and about the disabled car, and told her to call the police. We needed them right away.

Have you ever tried to cross four lanes of a major highway through heavy traffic? People in Massachusetts do not stop for breakdowns, accidents, or pedestrians; most people are on a mission. In all fairness, a lot of times, it's too dangerous to stop; a phone call to the police is best. But that day, I felt like the frog in the classic video game Frogger.

I was running very fast, but the cars were coming fast. I'd dodge one thinking I had plenty of time and then the next vehicle was on top of me. I finally made it to the other side, cars rushing past me, horns blaring at me, and jumped over the median strip guard rail.

"Are you OK?" I had to yell over the traffic noise.

She was frantic and rolled down her window, crying hysterically, "My car broke down and just shut off. I pulled as far as I could to the left because I was in the middle of the expressway and couldn't move to the right."

Unfortunately, she had inadvertently blocked herself in because she was right up against the guardrail on the left and trapped. She couldn't exit the passenger side door because she would be killed by traffic. It was a nightmare. If you've ever been broken down on the highway, you know how everything is so loud and so fast and so volatile. Cars were swerving just in time to avoid her car after they crested a small hill just before the Route 44 exit. A very confusing situation that needed focus and swift action.

I looked around. Not a lot of choices to be made. I said, "Roll down your window all the way, and I'll help you get out of the car. We'll wait for the police on the opposite side, away from traffic."

"But what about my kids!" she said, her eyes wide.

Kids? What kids?

I was so focused on this poor woman and so distracted by the cars swerving and just missing her car that I didn't see the two young boys in the back, who were probably two and four. Things just got compounded times a hundred, and I had to act with full intent and massive action. I pulled mom from the driver's seat window, and she then asked the four-year-old to unbuckle his brother and pass him out of the back seat window. My biggest mistake.

I should've left her in the car and had her pass the kids to me. I knew that they might not come to some stranger on the highway grabbing at them. He was just a scared boy whom his mom was giving away. When he realized what was happening due to our behavior and yelling, the four-year-old froze in fear. He wanted his mom even though she was right there on the other side of the window. I was afraid it was just a matter of time before her car would be rear-ended.

We yelled, "Roll the window down and hand me your brother! Please! Roll the window down!" I was yelling because time was critical and the traffic noise was loud. She was yelling out of extreme fear for their lives.

I grabbed a large rock from the ground and yelled, "Close your eyes!" I put the rock through the rear window. I knocked the fragments of the shatterproof glass out of the frame. I grabbed the young man by the shirt and begged him to unbuckle his brother and hand him to me. I looked deep into his soul as I instructed him sternly what I needed from him at that moment. By then, it was almost fully dusk; drivers had their headlights on, and it was becoming more difficult to see.

It was like a light went on in his head. He jumped out of his car seat and unbuckled his brother, who was screaming, "Mommy! Mommy! I want you!" He passed the toddler over to me; I handed him to his mom and carefully pulled the other boy out the window. Right after his feet cleared the door frame, a black car smashed into the back of the car pushing it down the guardrail for ten or fifteen feet and knocking the rear bumper into the middle of Route 3. Metal scraping, tires screeching, babies crying, cars still flying by. Noise. More noise. Total chaos. I grabbed the boy and rolled to the ground trying to cover him from any debris since I didn't really know exactly what was happening. I opened my eyes and realized we were all OK. I asked the mom, "Are you OK? What about the little guy?"

She stared at me speechless from fear of what could've happened. The four-year-old quickly escaped my bear hug and ran to his mother.

The police showed up right after the accident. In somewhat of a shock myself, I explained what had happened, and they directed me safely back across the expressway and into my car. Off I went to my girlfriend's house. I was shaking as I came down from whatever the hell had just happened. I didn't even find out the names of the people in the car. I just drove away.

When I got to Tina's, I told her what had happened and broke down in tears. The adrenaline swooped through me, and I was shaking with its effects. For weeks, I played it over and over in my head— how I should've done things different or more efficiently. But I was alive, and most important, the kids and their mom were alive and safe. I recognized after that whole incident when I had time to come down that it all could've played out very differently. The thought was horrifying. Every single hour, every single minute, every single second of that day was planned perfectly for the rescue to occur. Some say coincidence, some say universe, but I say destiny. It was a beautiful day to save lives. I was happy to have been be available to the universe and this family.

Chapter 9

Charlie's Problem Becomes
My Problem

W E WERE TAKING ON HEAVY fire on this heavily wooded ridge
line. We had no place to go. John, our weapons specialist, was
on the M60—an extremely powerful automatic weapon called the
Pig due to its size and appetite for ammunition. John was laying down
suppressive fire, and we were running short on ammo. The Pig could
fire between 500 and 650 rounds per minute. Ammunition was usually
fed into the weapon from a 100- or 250-round belt.

It was getting dark. It was cold, rainy, wet. We were hungry. We
had been out on this mission since the early morning without any
downtime or food. The only other thing that could be worse would
be if we were tired. And we were. We had been waiting for a while
on a sitrep (a situation report of a military situation) while holding our
ridge line position quietly until we were engaged by enemy fire. We
didn't know who it was or where they had come from, but we knew
that we had a situation that probably included casualties caused by these
possible rebels.

Night vision and previous intel speculated a group of possibly
ten armed with automatic weapons and a rocket-propelled grenade
(RPG), a shoulder-fired weapon that launches a rocket equipped with
an explosive warhead. Most RPGs can be carried by a single soldier.

We had no choice but to engage and give away our position.

Brian, one of our finest from the Third Ranger Battalion, was
bringing up the rear with Dog, our MPC (multipurpose canine), and

we hoped some hot soup. These MPC breeds were chosen because they were very aggressive, smart, loyal, and athletic. Brian, an average-sized soldier, was fit and funny as hell, and Dog was a beautiful, long, sleek, and lean German shepherd. Both had the balls of a brass monkey. Brian was one of the best soldiers I'd ever met, and I trusted him completely. This is the guy you wanted to be in the foxhole with—highly intelligent, skilled, but never short of a joke or prank.

He walked up and down the ridge line asking if we wanted hot soup. "Where the hell did you get hot fucking soup? What? No coffee?" asked Timmy, our forward observer.

In Brian's typical fashion, he laughed and said, "Don't worry. Have some."

Man, did it hit the spot. Nothing like sipping hot soup in the middle of hell ducking hot rounds flying over your head. By then, it was completely dark especially in the thick woods, and things had settled down primarily due to lack of visibility. It was time to move quickly and quietly.

The sitrep came in over the radio; Jim, our radio man, pulled us in as John continued to monitor with the Pig and night vision. Jim listened to the radio and then spoke succinctly. "We have an RPG-downed Blackhawk with multiple casualties. Zero details on the extent of the injuries or number dead. We have grid coordinates but no radio contact. We need to move."

We had limited pyro and limited ammo, but this is what we did as a team and typically how we rolled. Pyrotechnics range from flares to signals meant to communicate and illuminate as well as protect from advanced weapon systems.

No one gets left behind. We were going in. We backed down the ridge line and met at a rally point to map out our plan of entry. Our goal was to get there before the enemy and if needed take the fight to the enemy first and complete the rescue mission ... alive.

"Game on, fuckers. Let's go!" John rumbled.

We could always count on John, cigarette hanging out of his mouth, hat on sideways like a gangster, laughing as he always had a comment.

"Give me the green light, 'cause I'm ready to go," said Timmy.

We started moving in based on our grid coordinates about half a mile through rugged terrain and dense woods. We planned an exit strategy that was en route to a nearby mobile field hospital known as DEPMEDS (deployable medical systems). The problem was that we didn't know what kind of rebel enemy we may encounter or what kind of casualties we would be dealing with. Worse, we didn't know if we would have to carry bodies out. The wet and woody terrain made it quite impossible to be swift and quiet, but so far so good as we honed in on our objective.

We had the Blackhawk in sight. It was a mess. It looked like a bunch of scrap metal sitting in a ravine. We could hear moaning and some movement from the cockpit and the perimeter of the Blackhawk, but it was hard to see any details even with night vision; cold rain was beating on our heads.

Rat tat tat tat tat tat! Tracer rounds lit up the night sky and were coming in hot in our direction. We took cover. We knew it wasn't friendly fire as we had Jim radio in our location and coordinates. We were the only team in place carrying this mission out. It was showtime.

We threw a flare down in the hole of this ravine to light it up and see what we had. John set up the tripod for the Pig to cover us. Our team of five moved with purpose using obstacles of nature so we could get down into the chopper without being exposed.

The hum of bullets sounds like a million zip lines going by simultaneously. In this rush and hyper-focused time, wondering if one of those bullets might hit you was not a concern. Incendiary grenades burning and smoke screens for cover. Mission first.

We knew John had our six as he always did. (The saying originated with World War I fighter pilots referencing the rear of an airplane as the six o'clock. Now, it is a term in the military that highlights loyalty in the military culture. In other words, I got you covered.) You could always tell the difference of a .60 round coming out of the chamber. We had two soldiers and the pilot all with varying injuries.

One soldier wandered around the crash site confused and trying to help his comrades. He was bleeding from the head and had multiple lacerations on his face. The pilot was stuck in his seat and appeared to be in and out of consciousness. Though it was hard to see, the last soldier was bleeding from the head and had a partially amputated leg. This was a mess.

Brian and I did our quick medical assessments to triage, establish airways, and stop any massive blood loss just so we knew we could move these soldiers without causing more harm. We were able to quickly extract the pilot who had lost consciousness completely and the soldier who was clearly missing his right leg midcalf down. We performed our medic skills with intent and with perfection as we were trained so we could roll. "Time to move, gang! We gotta go! Brian, you good? I got one. You take one."

We quickly put the patients' arms over shoulders and put our fireman carries from boot camp back to work. We hustled up through the trees dragging our one ambulatory soldier by the arm blood dripping from his face diluted by the pouring rain. Then it was exit time. Our team prided ourselves on staying fit mentally and physically for any situation, and this was no different. We trained as we fought—we moved stealthily led by Dog with no compromise to our fellow injured soldiers. Hustling through the wet woods in what was then pouring rain watching the tracer rounds light up the night sky … heads down … running.

After what seemed like an eternity, we reached the open field where the field hospital was. We had radioed ahead with a sitrep on the wounded and potential injuries we had assessed. Doctors, surgeons, and medical personnel waited for us inside the security perimeter.

"Great job, guys. We got this from here," said the lead triage nurse.

I said, "This guy needs help. Tourniquet was placed forty-five minutes ago, and the pilot looks like impact wounds with a TBI (traumatic brain injury)."

We laid the severely injured soldier and pilot on cots as the nurses and doctors took over quickly. We were winded and drenched with our weapons and gear strapped to our bodies. The nurses laid our ambulatory soldier down as well since he had become quite disoriented by the time we had reached the tent.

"Good luck and Godspeed, gentleman," said Brian. "You're in capable hands, and they'll get you out of here safely."

More cold, more wet, more tired, and more hungry, we nonetheless performed an after-action performance review on our team and tried to decide if this was a scenario we wanted to utilize further in our training.

This luckily had been a training exercise for us despite using live rounds overhead to simulate the real deal. The downed Blackhawk scenario was one of many other mass-casualty incidents we implemented to be developed for special operations training and all medical groups of the military.

Our team called this lanes training, and it was known as the elite medical and tactical training for the military hosted by our team at Fort Devens, Massachusetts. The training also incorporated the setup and breakdown of the DEPMEDS, the new mobile hospital system. It was a complete functioning hospital with intensive care units, operating rooms, emergency triage rooms, radiology with CT scanner, and heat and air conditioning, and it was designed to be set up in two to three days and broken down just as fast. It was newly designed by the military, and it was a phenomenal system to have mobile and ready to deploy anywhere in the world at a moment's notice. It typically held between 44 and 248 hospital beds. Ideally, it would function as the bridge between incoming helicopter ambulances and outgoing air force aircraft.

DEPMEDS was very systematic; everything had to be done perfectly by the books as instructed. If it was done wrong, the entire system would fail and continue to pose problems during the installation. Our team, the best, became the trainers for the entire 94th Army Command; all military units came to train with us and participate in lanes training. We were awarded many a coin from visiting generals and many commendations from our units. (A commander's coin is a tangible way for senior military to honor staffers' exceptional achievements.)

I loved serving my country; I was a true patriot. The military gave me purpose, kept me sharp, and brought the most amazing team of men into my life to which I owe my life. Along with my dedication to God, country, and team, I also believed in upholding the Combat Medic's Creed.

The Medic Creed

My task is to provide to the utmost limits of my capability
the best possible care to those in need of my aid and assistance.

To this end I will aid all those who are needful,
paying no heed to my own desires and wants; treating friend,
foe and stranger alike, placing their needs above my own.

To no person will I cause or permit harm to befall,
nor will I refuse aid to any who seek it.

I will willingly share my knowledge
and skills with all those who seek it.

I seek neither reward nor honor for my efforts
for the satisfaction of accomplishment is sufficient.

These obligations I willingly and freely take upon
myself in the tradition of those that have come before me.

These things we do so that others may live.

The Medic's Creed. This is what medics do,
and I wanted to be second to none.

Another training exercise I participated in ended up a beautiful day to save lives. I had been home from Bosnia since the late spring. In the summer of 1996, also at Fort Devens, I had been sent to be the medic in charge for a very large training exercise for multiple units that were being graded by the upper echelons to assess deployment readiness for worldly conflicts. I had my ambulance and two young, inexperienced medics who honestly were just putting in their time.

This was a weeklong training exercise; I had very specific instructions from the commanding officer (CO) that the medical presence was strictly for show, what we called a dog-and-pony show. Show up and be present, but all medical issues or what we called sick call were to be sent to the medical center. He was adamant that there would be zero field medicine practiced.

I made sure that my days were spent bringing my two medics up to speed on their education and skills necessary not only for medical needs but also to become part of a team in which tactical soldier skills might be needed.

The week was terribly slow, and it had been super hot and dry all week out in the field, the kind of days during which you didn't do anything and you still wanted to shower at the end of it, but in the field, we could shower only every third day. It was dusty, and the air was thick and humid. The good news was that we had two days left of supporting this mission, and we were excited to be moving on to something more exciting and more motivating back at our home unit— the 309th Combat Support "Cash" Hospital based in Boston.

I was all push-upped out and was getting myself situated in the back of the ambulance that afternoon going over inventory when Charlie arrived. Charlie was a young female soldier about age twenty who was brought to me in acute respiratory distress. She looked fatigued; her face was dirty, and she looked ready to pass out. I saw her struggling to take short breaths. The soldiers who brought her to the ambulance had no idea what was happening; they were afraid to do anything to hurt—or help—her. They were part of an engineering unit, so not much to report about how this may have happened. She was walking but clearly tired. She had her hand across her chest, and her breathing was labored. "She just started having a hard time breathing," said one of the soldiers who had brought her over. "We didn't know what to do."

Apparently, she'd waited about twenty minutes before telling anyone about her breathing difficulties, and the clock was ticking. She could barely get a breath in or say anything. She had audible stridor, a narrowing of the upper airway; it's a high-pitched wheezing sound caused by disrupted airflow. Some people call it musical breathing or extra thoracic airway obstruction. Airflow is usually disrupted by a blockage of the voice box or windpipe. Her pulse was very high in conjunction with her blood pressure. Her oxygen saturation was starting to decrease when I put the pulse oximeter on her. Charlie was breathing rapidly and clearly using her accessory upper chest muscles to take in the small amount of air she was receiving versus the normal typical diaphragmatic breaths all of us take.

I had my team pick her up into the ambulance and lay her down so I could go to work. At that point, she was slipping into confusion and on her way to unconsciousness.

"Charlie, my name is Sergeant Miller, and I *will* take care of you.

Do you know of any past medical history in your family that would be important to know? Has this ever happened to you before?"

Charlie mumbled as best she could, "I'm ... allergic ... to grass ... and pollen," she wheezed. Medics referred to that as hay fever, which people typically experience as a runny nose, watery eyes, and sneezing. Clearly, Charlie had had a very severe allergic reaction that she had either never experienced before or opted to not disclose. How the hell does anyone get through a thorough military physical upon entry without coming clean about that type of allergy? But that didn't matter just then. It was time for me to do a thorough Brett brain review and decide on treatment options.

Anaphylaxis occurs most often in young people and females. As respiratory arrest starts, carbon dioxide isn't removed properly from the bloodstream, which causes a buildup of carbonic acid. Eventually, oxygen levels in the bloodstream diminish, and that can lead to problems in the brain and heart. Without treatment, respiratory arrest always leads to cardiac arrest.

Got it, Miller? You were made for this.

But wait ... That order from the CO: "There is to be no medical treatment whatsoever during this exercise under no circumstances. Do I make myself clear?" I was under his rank and command; my job was to not change orders but to follow them. I had to follow the chain of command. But Charlie was slipping into unconsciousness and was in full respiratory distress that would lead to cardiac arrest, and she could die in the back of my ambulance.

Along with the military chain of command doctrine, there's another famous credo among combat medics working in special operations: "Not on my watch." It was a beautiful day to save lives like every day for me, and Charlie was not dying on my watch no matter what the orders were. I would withstand all the consequences that I deserved.

I ordered one of my medics into the driver's seat. "Get me to the nearest hospital double time!"

My other medic became my tech. I asked for equipment none of which we had under the circumstances. Exasperated, I ordered, "See If you can find an IV kit with a fat gauge needle and some saline. I also need an ambu bag if there's one buried somewhere."

The medic just looked at me and started to cry.

"I know we have nothing. I've got this," I said. "Everything's going to be fine."

She managed to find an IV kit, which was a good start.

I slammed an IV in as fast as my hands allowed and ran fluids as quickly as possible. Most cases of anaphylaxis cause very low blood pressure. I had in my personal first aid kit some epinephrine, which could buy us some time. "Grab that emergency kit sitting between the front seats. Open it up and hand me the epinephrine pen."

I jammed that needle into Charlie's thigh and emptied the syringe as quickly as her quad would accept the medicine. The poor medic with me sat there frozen as she watched me push breaths from my mouth into Charlie's airway. She stopped breathing. Due to the constriction of her throat and swelling of her tongue, I was meeting a lot of resistance. I kept repositioning her head in hopes of see her chest rise like those stupid dummies we practiced with. It wasn't happening.

I tried again. Head tilt, chin lift, pinch the nose, and blow. That time, I felt some air go in. Alas, right into her stomach because immediately Charlie vomited into my mouth. *Fuck!* I'd been warned that might happen.

"Roll her to me! She's vomiting!" I shouted to the poor, scared medic. I swiped her airway using my fingers to empty the chunks of vomit out of her mouth as we took a sharp left, and I almost fell over in the ambulance. "Drive faster! We gotta go! I have nothing!"

Charlie still wasn't breathing. We were losing time. Pulse check … Nothing. Check again … Nothing. Charlie unfortunately had followed the protocol: with no treatment, patient will experience cardiac arrest. There I was on my watch with a twenty-something-year-old in my care not breathing and with no pulse. Medically termed dead. And in my ambulance. I wasn't having it not only for my moral obligation as a medic but more important for this poor girl who had a family and the rest of her life to live.

Fifteen compressions … Two breaths … Fifteen compressions … Two breaths … Fifteen compressions … Two breaths. This was before CPR procedures had changed and before the age of automatic external defibrillator devices. Man, I was tired, and I was in only my first round.

Please come alive. Please come alive.

Nothing.

"We're here!" shouted my medic driver.

"Pull right up to the front door!"

I did my last set of compressions and breaths, slammed the back ambulance door open, and carried her lifeless body into the ER. My assistant medic carried the bag of fluids. It was like carrying Eric all the way up that hill that day to the nurse's office at music camp. And all too familiar.

"She's dead. I need your help!"

A whole team came rushing out, and we threw her onto a gurney. I trotted next to her into the hospital. I kept breathing for her and compressing her. It was like I was looking down at myself working—an out-of-body experience just doing what I was taught all by myself.

The team of doctors dismissed me quickly in the treatment bay; they had the necessary equipment to work efficiently on her. They also told me I could not stay. I understood.

We had called Central Command back on the base to give them the sitrep, and I was asked to return to the base immediately. I knew this was not going to be good.

I entered the typical brick building with the cookie-cutter architecture common to all military installations. I was greeted by a young specialist who asked if I was Sergeant Miller.

I was set to meet with the command sergeant major (CSM), a senior noncommissioned rank, the highest enlisted rank and the senior enlisted advisor to the commanding officer. CSMs serve as monitors and advocates for enlisted soldiers.

I was like, *Great ... Everyone knows who I am today.* I was told to sit and wait by this door. It was just like those days outside the principal's office except that time, I was in real-life trouble and I knew it. The fifteen minutes that went by seemed like an eternity.

A stern voice that carried through the whole building called out, "Sergeant Miller, please enter." I walked in head high and stood at parade rest. There was CSM Guarino squinting through his glasses. He was a little guy sitting at his desk with feet up and cigar smoke caressing his face. "What the hell do you think you're doing? You had strict orders to follow!"

I was professional and intact whenever I needed to be, but I still had some good old smart-ass left in me. "Saving lives, Sergeant Major. These are the things medics do so that others may live." Not too smart, but boy, that felt good. And quoted right from the Medic's Creed.

After being chewed out very loudly by a very small man who didn't look capable of producing such loud noises, I was pulled off the training exercise and put up in the barracks for the last night of training. The CSM also reminded me that this would be reported to my superiors at my home unit and that they would decide the appropriate discipline and action to take.

I considered myself lucky. I wasn't punished under the Uniform Code of Military Justice, and I didn't lose my rank as sergeant. I walked out of that brick building that day with head up and big grin on my face. "Fuck off," I muttered under my breath and carried on.

The next day concluded the training exercise, and all the units returned to base for debriefings, after-action reviews, a closing ceremony, and a formal dismissal. I made sure I made my way across the field to speak with the officer in charge of the unit Charlie belonged to to see if anyone knew what was the result.

He told me that she had survived anaphylaxis brought on by her allergy to pollen and grass that hadn't been disclosed during her formal army physical. Due to the CPR that I had performed on her, she had had a pulse upon admission to the hospital; it was just too slow and weak to actually palpate. The injection of epinephrine was also life-saving because it bought us some time to get to the hospital. Her respiratory arrest and consequent cardiac arrest was delayed long enough so that Charlie wouldn't have any long-term effects from anoxia. She was still in the hospital and was to be discharged that afternoon to head back to her home.

I never got a chance to see Charlie again, but I'm sure she was grateful, and I hoped she didn't remember any of the incident. I did find out that they planned on giving her a medical discharge.

When I returned to my home unit, word of the incident had already reached my superiors, and to my surprise, I was awarded the Army Commendation Medal for saving someone's life. That hot, steamy day … It was for Charlie. *Oorah!*

It was a beautiful day to save lives.

DEPARTMENT OF THE ARMY
THIS IS TO CERTIFY THAT THE SECRETARY OF THE ARMY HAS AWARDED

THE ARMY COMMENDATION MEDAL

TO SERGEANT BRETT ANDREW MILLER

FOR EXCEPTIONAL PERFORMANCE OF DUTY DURING A LIFE THREATENING SITUATION.
SGT MILLER PROVIDED EXEMPLARY CARE TO THE PATIENT WHICH IN FACT SAVED HER LIFE.
SGT MILLER IS A CREDIT TO HIMSELF, THE 309th COMBAT SUPPORT HOSPITAL AND THE
UNITED STATES ARMY RESERVE.

GIVEN UNDER MY HAND IN THE CITY OF WASHINGTON
THIS   3RD   DAY OF   NOVEMBER   19 96

THOMAS J. MULVANEY
COL. MC, USAR
COMMANDING

PERMANENT ORDER #11-107

DA FORM 4980-14, APR 81

The Army Commendation Medal I received for saving Charlie's life

Chapter 10

The Armor Got Too Heavy

I N 1996, I COMPLETED MY last mission for the army. I spent two weeks with NATO in Bosnia, Skopje, Macedonia, and Albania trying to facilitate faster and safer evacuations in conjunction with hospital triaging. This was in preparation to care for all the land mine explosions of civilians and injuries caused by the never-ending religious war. The standard of care and the facilities for surgery were less than adequate. The surgical areas were open rooms that typically would be used for overnight stays in a hospital in the United States. The sterilization equipment was simply stainless-steel kitchen bowls with archaic surgical tools.

It was supposedly a peaceful, humanitarian NATO mission aligned with the Geneva Conventions, but the rules of engagement with other countries didn't always apply. The Geneva Conventions were a series of four treaties negotiated in 1949 after World War II that established the standards of international law for humanitarian treatment in war. It defined the rights of civilians and military personnel to protect them in and around a war zone. Under the Geneva Conventions, the Red Cross emblem was intended to protect and identify medical and relief workers, military and civilian medical facilities, and mobile units and hospital ships during armed conflict. Although the Geneva Conventions document has no provisions for punishment, violations typically lead to trade sanctions and moral outrage against the offending government.

Luckily, our military translator and driver bent the rules unbeknown to us, and that saved our lives in Albania. It's heavily frowned upon to be carrying weapons across a border and particularly in a NATO vehicle on a humanitarian mission. This was another solo mission for me; my training team wasn't present. Army Command had chosen me to represent the US Army for professional development and lead medical advice. I was honored, but my armor was getting heavy by that time.

I was weighed down with the accumulation of my varied experiences in the streets of Macedonia, Croatia, and at that time, Albania. I was proud and honored to be chosen to be part of such an amazing humanitarian project, but I spent many nights staring at the ceiling with anxiety and sleeplessness from experiences that these poor people suffered through. I was obsessed by the terrible treatment these people suffered—the civilian deaths, children dying and maimed and traumatized ... The massacres are still something no one talks about to this day, but one of the largest massacres in history had taken place. All that shit was adding up and I was absorbing it myself., I felt I was carrying it all in my rucksack, in my med supply duffel, in my armor. I was weighed down by many feelings.

We drove across the border into Albania on a humanitarian mission as Albanian forces worked alongside NATO forces in peacekeeping operations in Bosnia and Herzegovina. Albania also played an important role in supporting allied efforts to end the humanitarian tragedy in Kosovo and secure the peace after the air campaign. However, Albania had its own issues in 1996 as it was revving up for the Albanian rebellion of 1997, when the government was toppled and more than 2,000 were killed. There were still many Albanian rebels in hiding, and groups were conducting kidnappings and executions.

As a NATO escorted team, we didn't intend to cross paths or have any interaction with those groups. Colonel Tom Mulvey and Staff Sergeant Sara Fonte rode with me as part of the European collaboration until we realized we were being followed. We had left Skopje, Macedonia, and were headed to Tirana, the capital of Albania, but we never made it. I had noticed our driver, who didn't speak English, kept looking at the rearview mirror nervously. There was a lot of back-and-forth chatter between the driver and our translator.

"Listen," the translator said to me and the other two military people with us, "we think we're being followed. Don't turn around. Let's see if we can ride this out."

Ride this out? Are you fucking kidding me? Ride this out? Where the hell are we? Can we radio for help?

There I was without my team on a solo mission with no weapons. I had no idea where I was. It was supposed to be a friendly mission. I couldn't communicate with our driver, and we were being followed by what I presumed were rebels who I could guarantee were armed, dangerous, and no respecters of life. It was a known fact that NATO vehicles were peacekeeping vehicles that traveled typically unarmed. I figured I'd be executed if we were stopped or kidnapped, tortured, and put up for ransom. The Albanian rebels' reputation preceded them. They were known for their barbaric ways and their great dislike for Americans.

"Move over," our translator said. "Get out of the way."

I had no idea what he was up to until he flipped the bench seat up and I saw a rack of five 9 mm handguns with loaded clips. A beautiful sight. He handed one to me. "Here. They're loaded."

"Sweet Jesus, I might have a shot at living today!" A little Brian humor in the midst of a world of shit. Boy, was I missing my regular team. The driver sped up while conversing with the translator. He was sweating as he carelessly drove down old, not maintained, hilly, and curvy country roads.

Mulvey and Fonte, who were also medical consultants, were practically under their seats hiding especially because they were sitting in the rear of the vehicle closest to the back windshield.

"Colonel, do you know how to shoot one of these nines? Sergeant?" I asked. You guessed it—the deer in the headlights look.

"Not since we last qualified on the range," said Tom. *Shit. Officers.*

Fontes said nothing; I saw that she was full of fear and quietly weeping.

We're fucked. What would John do? What would the team do? The last thing I wanted was to engage these people. We didn't know who they were, why they were following us, or what type of arsenal they might have in their vehicle. We had five pistols and only two people capable of using them—the translator and me. As our driver picked up speed, so did the other vehicle.

"Can we lose them somehow?" I was unfamiliar with the terrain but thought if we could at least get some distance between us we could disappear somewhere in the countryside and wait it out. "It's probably our best option, don't you think?"

"Yes," said the translator as he went back and forth in two languages with the driver and me. "I feel it's our only option."

I loaded the first round into the chamber of my weapon and took it off safety. *Click, click* went the slide. I wanted to snap my fingers and be home. I started praying, something I always did before any of my missions with the boys. I heavily relied on my faith; I carried a miniature version of the Bible in my fatigues so I could look up short prayers based on my emotions and feelings at that specific time.

> Even though I walk through the valley of the shadow of death, I will fear no evil, for you are with me; your rod and your staff, they protect me. You prepare a table before me in the presence of my enemies; you anoint my head with oil; my cup overflows. Surely goodness and mercy shall follow me all the days of my life.

We were driving very fast on the winding roads of Albania. Large areas of beautiful green pasture and farmland covered the landscape. I turned sidesaddle on the bench seat and carefully placed my weapon on the top of the seat facing directly at the driver who was following us. My hands were shaking. Lucky for us, the windows were tinted so I couldn't be seen.

I frequently had been the range safety officer or the weapons instructor during weapon qualifications for the 9 mm handgun at Fort Devens. I'd also learned a lot just from hanging with John and the team for so many years, but typically, the words *weapons* and *combat medics* were never in the same sentence except in special operations.

"If I can take the driver out or at least shatter the windshield, we should have an opportunity to find cover," I said.

I knew from my training that shooting into glass was always a dicey proposition. The angle of the glass in relation to me was the biggest factor that would determine the impact of a bullet on the target. The rule of thumb was that when firing from outside into glass, the angle of a windshield will deflect a bullet downward; therefore, you typically aimed high. The problem I had was risking reaching out the window and exposing myself. That tactic would leave no room for error. I didn't want to shoot out our back window first and then try to hit the driver behind us.

I decided I would fill the windshield with holes as fast as I could so we could escape. Combat shooting and defensive measures were not my specialty; many scenarios played out in my mind. I was very scared and didn't know what to do. When I ran missions with the team, we always trained to control the situation, but I had no control this time.

My driver slammed on the brakes and swerved abruptly. I almost fell out of my seat. "Yo!" I yelled and turned sharply. Out of the front windshield, I saw coming up a hill into a hard right turn an average-sized man wearing a *fustanella*, a traditional Albanian white kilt; a *tirqe*, long pants; and a long-sleeved jacket. His white hair and beard were scraggly. He looked scared and surprised; we were about to run him over. That along with all the other distractions our driver was facing ...

The man waved a long, thin stick at what I figured to be at least a hundred head of cattle across the street.

"Keep driving!" I yelled. "Keep going! Tell him to move!" Our driver understood my tone of voice if not specifically what I had said. He swerved around the poor farmer. We lurched left and then right and in between two cows and kept going. And then the group of rebels came up over the same hill and around the same corner except by that time, the cattle were ambling across the street heads down, without worry, just following the swinging tails of the cows ahead of them.

I still view that as a gift from God. It gave us enough time to create some distance and carry out our mission. It was like a scene from a movie; just at the last minute, a situation completely out of our control disrupted the action, and we got out of what could've been a deadly encounter. Once on the other side of the cattle and some distance away, we felt safer.

I put my elbows on my knees and my head in my hands and let

out the deepest exhalation ever. My body odor permeated through the armpits of my uniform. I was soaked. Sweat dripped off my eyelashes and onto my lips and tongue. Salty.

That was the first time I thought seriously about where I wanted to be in ten years with my career, family, and military duty. I had really thought that I wouldn't survive that day. I had never experienced such intense fear.

A week later, I boarded a plane at the Franjo Tudman Airport in Croatia and flew civilian flights home. I was still quite shaken up and not myself.

My discharge date of March 28, 1998, from the army was creeping up, and I had to make a crucial decision—family or country. Was I going to be on the move constantly running missions for the army, or was I going to continue to develop my physical therapy career and start a family?

With a lot of guilt and a lot of mixed emotions, I decided to leave my team and move forward in the next chapter of my life. I had talked and joked with the guys about moving on after that horrific scare in Albania. "The first sergeant and company commander are begging me to stay another eight years and are offering me a ten thousand dollar bonus. That would get me far," I told John.

He laughed. "You're a lifer, Miller. Shut up and sign the paperwork, you idiot. Plus, who the hell am I going to harass?"

We laughed it off, but in a quieter time, I talked to Brian about my decision. I respected his advice and always looked up to him as a leader in our team.

"Brian, I'm really thinking about hanging up the towel. I can't shake the anxiety that I've been dealing with since I got back, and I'm worried that I won't be able to enjoy having children or a wife if I'm always being called for service. I'm torn. Plus, I already feel guilty about leaving you guys hanging. It's a mess."

Brian was his usual casual self. "You'll figure it out, and you know how we feel about you. You're the man! You never let us down. We would always respect your decision, but we would never tell you we'd miss you." He laughed and put me in a headlock with noogie knuckles on the head.

"Fuck off!" I said, my usual response to most of their unconditional love, a man's true way of communicating through caring emotions—with profanity and laughter.

This was one of life's hardest decisions for me, and as I suspected, I paid the price. After I left, my entire 110 team was activated and entrenched in Iraq. TJ, my replacement, had half his face blown off by an IED along with a TBI (traumatic brain injury). That was something medics couldn't have prevented, but medics would *think* they could've prevented it if they had been there. The burden was heavy, and the armor continued to weigh me down. Guilt ran wild, and my former teammates suffered a tremendous amount of PTSD.

As bizarre as it sounds, we lost contact with each other as the years went on; we were suffering by ourselves in our own worlds and never knew it until we finally connected many years later.

By late 1998, I was living in Plymouth and working at Jordan Hospital, practicing physical therapy and moving up the ranks with a business mind my dad had instilled in me. I practiced in multiple settings and worked part time in a fitness center purely for the love of fitness and helping people recover from their injuries. Life was pretty good. I had a lot of great people in my life in business and pleasure, and I learned a lot about life from them. No one was going to lose a finger in my gym, and no one was going to die in my ambulance.

I enjoyed the break from the universe because though life was good, I had become hyper alert of my surroundings. If I went to church or any other large gathering, I assessed exits and profiled people constantly. I entered a room or building and always looked for the perfect cover in the case of an ambush, mental behavior that had been ingrained in me in the military, and there was no breaking that cycle. Deep breathing, yoga, meditation? I didn't have time for that kind of stuff, and I didn't think anything was wrong with being the way I was.

Instead, I found solace outside strengthening my relationship with Mother Nature. I enjoyed hiking and ice and rock climbing. The higher the elevation, the more invigorating. That was my church.

I met my lovely wife, Audrey, after returning from summiting Mount Kilimanjaro in 2000. We were caring for the same patient at the hospital where we worked. She was a traveling nurse and had two weeks left on her commitment before going home to Ohio.

We got married six months later, on May 23, 2001, on a 105-degree day on Roatán, an island off the coast of Honduras. What a beautiful place to get married. I had connections in Boston, and she was from Ohio and had eight siblings; we had a bash in Massachusetts and another in Ohio a couple of weeks apart. It was a month-long wedding full of family and fun.

Our married life began with amazing days in a great apartment in Hingham on the Weir River with some of our closest friends living downstairs. We could walk to World's End and enjoy all the trails and the Boston skyline views, or we could drop our kayaks in the river across the street and paddle to Nantasket Beach, where I had almost lost my friend Greg. It was a super place to live with all the amenities.

Two years later, we entered the next phase of life, which included buying a home in Hanson, a rural town twenty minutes from Hingham, and starting a family. I ventured into the business world when my partner and I started a medical supply business. He was a fantastic guy I knew from my position as a rehabilitation manager for many long-term care facilities. David ended up being my longtime friend, godparent to my twin sons, and great business partner for twenty years. He was a standup guy with a heart full of compassion; he believed in the adage that hard work and being a good guy win every time.

Our business, Boston Orthotics, designed and sold custom wheelchairs, braces, custom shoes, and orthotics as well as seating systems and strollers for children and adults on hospice services. It was an amazing business, and we prided ourselves on knowing our customers and their families. It was a true customer service business built on hard work and strong ethics.

We started in David's garage in 2002, graduated to a five-hundred-square-foot room in a bus station, and then moved on to multiple warehouses in multiple states. We had over thirty employees whom we treated like family, and they loved being a part of Boston Orthotics as did their families. We would often attend baseball games, cookouts, and holiday parties all together.

Audrey gave birth to Isabel Rose on February 21, 2005. She was the light of my life, and she still is. She had a beautiful soul and consistently happy disposition. Audrey and I were on top of the moon. Audrey's job as a nurse afforded her a lot of time off, and my work at Boston Orthotics afforded me a lot of flexibility so that one of us was always home with Isabel. We were very blessed.

My dad, who had become my best friend when I was a young adult, sat for hours with Isabel resting in his arms, sleeping, or playing. My dad enjoyed his favorite corner on our leather couch in our TV room, where he would sit and wait for Audrey or me to put Isabel in his arms. She was so content just sleeping. Unlike me, my dad had such patience and would just watch her breathing for hours at a time. Because she was a newborn, we would perfectly and tightly swaddle her, and she loved snuggling in my dad's arm and elbow, her little nest. He had no desire to get up; he was content just holding her, a beautiful display of affection and pride.

Becoming parents came with challenges I think strictly from naïveté, but with the three of us together, the universe brought such deep and vibrant love. At least until I, deemed by the universe as a healer always available to save lives, started fighting for my own life.

The armor was too heavy.

Audrey struggled intensely with postpartum depression. Even after working in health care as a physical therapist and actually teaching pre- and postnatal exercise classes, I had no idea of the impact such depression could have on a mother. I came home from work day after day and found Audrey sitting in the kitchen alone sobbing for no apparent reason. It was frustrating to know that there was nothing I could do especially with my mentality geared toward rescuing people from intense situations. She couldn't figure it out, but after about three months of professional help from her holistic friends and medical doctors, she rallied, and her depression dissipated. Thank God. What a horrible thing for anyone to deal with; you should be elated to have a baby rather than always wanting to cry.

I noticed I was running. Running from what I didn't know. Like most of us would, I ignored the physical and mental race I was in and focused on being overly busy and focused on supporting my family. I felt like a caged lion pacing back and forth and pausing at each corner looking out at the world and feeling frustrated, restless, and angry. Something was definitely off; I had always had a vision of a life that was more beautiful than mine at that time. I reminded myself to be grateful for my beautiful family and good health. It was wrong of me to desire something that didn't exist. I didn't know that I was running from success. I was the problem. My perspective was the problem.

The art of distraction—something human beings are proficient at. If I kept busy, I felt, I wouldn't have to think about my issues or take an inventory to see who was looking back at me in the mirror.

We all need a mission. Life should be a mission. It gives us purpose, it stimulates goals, it gives us focus and drive, and that gives our lives meaning. Your mission can be anything from achieving work goals, caring for your family, starting a business, or conquering the world. After spending years handling rescue missions and after spending eight years in the military always having and knowing my mission, I lost my mission, my purpose, and therefore my satisfaction in life.

And so for this warrior, my mission ended, and as is true for everyone in the military, it ends. Our job was to prepare for war and to fight the enemy and win. That's exactly what we did, and we trained as we fought. Excellence in practice, excellence in performance.

After I retired from the service, I began paying the price mentioned earlier. By 2008, I had lost my mission, and all the guilt, PTSD, and remorse for leaving my team ten years earlier simply surfaced. It was the most bizarre and intense sensation. I realize now that my issues had been there for some time but that I had done a great job stuffing them back down. My feelings or lack thereof were leading me down a dark, lonely, selfish, and self-centered path.

It started with intense amounts of anxiety and states of panic during which I thought I was dying. I had chest pains and felt that I couldn't breathe. My blood pressure went through the roof, and I had heart rates in the 200s. One incident I remember quite clearly.

I had just presented my business and the products and services we provided to a medical facility. While I was talking, I felt that I was short of breath, and my heart rate accelerated. I felt it pounding rapidly. *I have to get out of here.* My brain was telling me that I needed to escape; I was in an unexplained state of panic. That was very odd since I'd never been nervous in front of individuals or groups before.

I quickly finished my business and was able to get to my car. I started speeding home, where I felt I would be safe. I had no idea what was happening to my body, but I was smart enough to know that something medical could have been horribly wrong. I decided to map out the hospitals on my route home if I needed to find an emergency room.

I apprehensively called Audrey and told her what was going on. Being a nurse, she told me to get to an ER. Against her advice, I decided to drive on until I got to the point that I was unable to catch my breath and a sensation of impending doom overwhelmed me. *I think I'm going to die of a heart attack.* That made no sense medically because I was physically fit and young and I had no family history of cardiac issues. I was clearly out of my mind and therefore not making sense.

About twenty minutes from home, I did stop at a hospital and went into the ER. The nurse at the front desk asked, "Can I help you?" I probably looked pretty normal compared to most people who came to an ER.

"I can't breathe. I have chest pain, and I feel like my heart is coming out of my chest."

She immediately took my blood pressure—220/90—my pulse—182 bpm—and my respirations—twenty-five per minute. They immediately admitted me and kept me overnight to rule out a heart attack or any other acute illness. Nothing physical showed up. But yet I was so sick. I left the hospital with no clear answers.

Because of my strong desire to hold it together, my issue went unnoticed by my family and my business colleagues. I continued to work not wanting to admit anything was wrong, but I was uncomfortable in my skin all day. That led to my cutting my work days shorter and shorter. I was smoking cigarettes, drinking heavily, taking anxiety medication, drinking coffee, and exercising a lot. Sounds healthy, right?

That became my new normal for many years. I was the guy who always had a mission, who was always in the right place at the right time, always available for a beautiful day to save lives. But at that point, I was unable to support the heavy armor I was wearing. I was in the fight for my own life. The stress of family and being self-employed and the feelings of guilt left on the dirt roads of Macedonia and shame and remorse for having left my team came to a head and settled in my body. It was a perfect storm in which I was drowning slowly unable to bring my mouth to the surface for a breath.

After a few years of that lifestyle, my marriage starting falling apart, three-year-old Isabel wanted nothing to do with me, and I was clearly not working up to my potential. I owned two homes and three cars, I had money in the bank ... But I had nothing. I was drinking a thirty-pack of beer daily in conjunction with my antianxiety medicine just so I could get out of my head. I was performing nightly reconnaissance missions with a weapon; I was crawling in the yard around my house. I was paranoid about being ambushed by what, I did not know. Any noise I heard during my recon mission was considered someone or something that was coming for me. I had become afraid of the dark when it used to be my old friend. I was living in a state of constant fear and full-blown anxiety. What had happened?

Isolation, denial, addiction, sadness, and anger are what happened. My life was spiraling out of control. I was showing up at Alcoholics Anonymous meetings and for marriage counseling sessions but wasn't doing the work I needed to do—admission, recognition, moral inventory, humility, prayer, and forgiveness of self. I was too wrapped up in who I was supposed to be rather than who I was meant to be.

February 10, 2010, was a beautiful day to save lives. Except that day, someone saved mine.

Chapter 11

Someone Saved My Life Tonight

I T WAS A MAGNIFICENT WINTER day—bluebird sky, warm sunshine, and crisp air, one of those days when I could smell the winter. So pleasant, so beautiful, so relaxing. But I had just woken from yet another night of my daughter distancing herself from my wife and me because we had been yelling at each other about my problems. The armor had reached its limit; I could no longer support the weight bearing down on me, my soul, and my spirit. I had fully lost my mission.

I made a plan that night for my last day on earth.

I left early the next morning for work just like every morning except this time with one of my pistols and some ammunition. I drove up our long driveway emotionless as if I were driving off into the sunset at the end of a movie. Tears poured down my face. I had the feel of heavy armor on my body. I was missionless. I felt I was living a life of lies and expending useless amounts of energy to make things look normal and justifying it all to myself. I was exhausted, remorseful, and full of guilt and shame.

For some reason, I drove to an Alcoholics Anonymous meeting called the Early Bird. It started at seven for people who needed to get to a meeting before work. I had bounced in and out of there dozens of times shaking and sweating at seven in the morning just trying to put together a day of sobriety. That day was no different except I that I was nauseous and gagging my coffee down. I blamed it on the fact that I knew I couldn't do this anymore and had to get to a different place and stop hurting everyone around me. I felt I was in the third grade again

84

sitting behind that three-walled desk isolated, angry, careless, and cut off from the world.

I passed by the meeting place and sat in my van way down at the end of Route 18 in a town called Abington. Parking was allowed on the side along the road, and I held my weapon on my lap. It was locked and loaded and shaking in my hand. I had made sure I'd chosen the .357 Magnum with a hollow pointed bullet to assure my death from a gunshot into my mouth and through my brain stem. Well researched of course by my obsessive-compulsive self. I thought about all the damage I had caused others, how much I had embarrassed them and myself, my inefficient efforts at work, failure at fatherhood, and all the selfishness behind suicide.

My phone rang. *Why now? Why should I answer it?*

It was Paul, a friend I had met a while ago at that early morning meeting. "I saw you drive by. Are you coming in to the meeting?"

I was staring into nothingness through the windshield. I held my weapon in my white-knuckled hand. "Paul, things are bad. I don't think I'm coming in again … Ever."

Paul got serious. "Listen, man, you don't ever have to do this again. Put the drink down. You don't have to wake up every single day shakin', rattlin', and rollin'. You don't ever have to be alone again. Just come walk through the door. We're here at the meeting. Just walk in and have a cup of coffee."

I respected Paul. He had had a lot of sobriety time.

"Brett? You know that I've been there and that I've hit bottom too, but you know this commitment is just one day at a time. Let's just do today. Let's just do now. Just put the drink down for today. Come have a cup of coffee. You don't have to do this ever again. You never have to be alone again. Think about your family. Just one day. Do the next right thing, Brett."

You don't ever have to do this again. You never have to be alone again. Those two sentences and my friend Paul, to whom I am forever indebted, saved my life that day.

"OK," I said. "OK, I will. Just for today." I put the pistol in the glove compartment, wiped the tears from my bloodshot eyes and reddened face, and drove back to the meeting.

Since that day, February 10, 2010, I've never had the urge to pick up a drink. A spiritual awakening or the grace of God? I call it supernatural favor. I believed that the universe and its higher powers could restore my sanity. What I could not do on my own, the universe would make happen for me ... Supernatural opportunities including healing, restoration, vindication, freedom, and victorious breakthroughs would come to me if I listened and was self-aware.

I would come to discover talents I didn't know I had, and I would accomplish my universe-given dreams and ultimately my destiny. When I thought about all those days of saving lives in every fashion, I recognized the impact the universe had on my destiny. The understanding of giving my will and power away to the universe. Letting go as some might say. For me, it was finally taking off my heavy armor that once weighed me down almost to death and finding a new mission. That mission became vivid when I became quiet and reengaged with life.

This new life definition was not easy by any means; it took a lot of work just to scratch the surface of every emotional thread involved. Thread by thread, I found meaning and purpose as to why what had happened to me had happened. It meant a lot of hitting my knees in prayer and a lot of staying connected initially to stay sober. I started getting honest with myself and my family as the days went by, and that was painful and invigorating at the same time. I had come clean with my wife about hiding alcohol, why I did what I did when I did whatever I did, the continuous blackouts, and the lies associated with my actions. I attended a men's group on Wednesday nights to discuss similarities in our disease behaviors and actions and to sort through the whys and what fors.

Naturally, I felt better physically, mentally, and spiritually. My wife wanted to talk to me again, and my Isabel was back in my life as a daughter should be at that age cuddling and looking up to a strong father figure. The days of my Isabel wanting to be with her dad instead of pushing away or avoidance were on again. The nightly book reading, once a time of connection and bonding, had resumed. I started to redefine my life balance of family and work and life on life's terms. Reloaded, reengaged, reenlisted in life. Learning to remember why I had started this journey and living by the creed I swore I would always uphold.

The Medic Creed

**My task is to provide to the utmost limits of my capability
the best possible care to those in need of my aid and assistance.**

**To this end I will aid all those who are needful,
paying no heed to my own desires and wants; treating friend,
foe and stranger alike, placing their needs above my own.**

**To no person will I cause or permit harm to befall,
nor will I refuse aid to any who seek it.**

**I will willingly share my knowledge
and skills with all those who seek it.**

**I seek neither reward nor honor for my efforts
for the satisfaction of accomplishment is sufficient.**

**These obligations I willingly and freely take upon
myself in the tradition of those that have come before me.**

These things we do so that others may live.

The Medic's Creed

I had the joy of spending days seeing life through an infant's eyes. Although I was on a pink cloud floating on this new life, there was still a lot of cleaning up to do on my side of the road ... not taking anyone's inventory and being less critical and judgmental.

One of my and my family's most satisfying accomplishments was having my wife present me with my one-year medallion for sobriety. In February 2011, Audrey stood at the podium in the AA meeting room looking beautiful and resolute and so proud of me. Her voice shook a little as she started.

"For those of you who don't know me, I am Brett's wife, a nurse, and a mother. I am proud and honored to be able to give him this one-year medallion tonight. One year ago, I thought that I was going to be a single mother and that my daughter was going to grow up without a father. I even called a friend of mine, a neurosurgeon. I didn't know why my husband's behavior had drastically changed. He was losing his balance nightly practically falling and forgetting things. I thought he had a brain tumor. He had hidden his alcohol from Isabel and me for such a long time."

I had been in hiding for a long time wasting energy to keep my real disease away from the world. Burying it. Internalizing it. Listening to her talk about her journey as she watched this man she was slowly losing was incredibly sad. Watching the daily deterioration of a soul once successful and full of life. This ceremony was a giant step for my family, who now believed I was finally moving in the right direction, refocused, and repurposed.

I met a wonderful therapist along the way whom a family friend had recommended to me. I spent almost two years seeing her privately in Cambridge. We were lucky to have the resources, and it was worth every cent. She used a technique called the Tapas acupressure technique (TAT), an alternative medicine therapy that claims to clear negative emotions and past trauma. This is a self-application of light pressure to four areas of the head while placing your attention on a series of verbal steps that release blockages and allow for healing. TAT was originally intended for allergy elimination, but the emphasis switched to dealing with emotional trauma.

My therapist believed I was suffering from PTSD that had resulted from my experiences leading up through my childhood and into my days in the military. We dug deep into the soul of Brett Miller during those appointments, but I felt so much clearer and spiritually free after our sessions that I was confidently sharing everything with her. She was a huge catalyst for my healing and had a profound impact on my recovery process.

Unfortunately, one of the most tragic things happened to me during that time. I am most grateful I was in the space I was in or I believe I would have been in a very disconnected, lonely world by myself. In March 2010, I lost my best friend of thirty years—my dad. He was my stepdad but to me a true dad. He had come into our lives in Norwell in our run-down home on King's Landing when we were young kids. He had adopted my brother and me and treated us with respect, like his own. My dad and I had become very close in my late teens, and this was beyond devastating for me.

I was literally unable to speak for a week, and I was unable to read at his formal military burial. I wrote something that I had planned to relate at his funeral about the hero who had saved my life and how he had been the wind beneath my wings all along, but I didn't even bring it to the service. I just could not speak.

My dad was a proud marine of the First Marine Division. He was buried at Bourne National Cemetery on Cape Cod on a cold but sunny day. The color guard emotionally and perfectly snapped and folded the flag of the United States of America and then presented it to my mom as "Taps" played solemnly in the distance. I couldn't pull it together without breaking down. It was the hardest thing I ever had to sift through, and it could have sent me careening back into isolation had I not been doing the soul work and healing restoration.

I was spending a lot of time on the road for my business and frequently had a lot of alone time in traffic and throughout my day in between customers to go through my healing process and think about how I had ended up in this space at that moment.

The universe had consistently presented me with situations that required me to act and respond selflessly for others' sakes and live a life that was worthy of being proud of. A beautiful family, homes, transportation, and a business owner. This is when I realized that God had given me so many additional alive days that I began to understand the true obligation I had to pay it back.

Back when I was armored and mission driven, if others had asked me what they should do if they lost their mission or needed a new mission or a new sense of drive, I would tell them to go help someone; doing so would help the person, help the universe, and ultimately help them redefine themselves and their mission. Helping others helps us stay the course and defines our mission, our passions, and our drives.

Every day is a beautiful days to save lives, especially if it's your own.

Chapter 12

The Comeback Is Always Better Than the Setback

T HEY SAY EVERYONE SHOULD TAKE their own breath away once to experience rebirth, regeneration, and repurpose. Becoming the victor and not the victim. As the days and years passed, I continued to do my hard, honest work daily—praying, helping others, and listening quietly for the moments when the universe would call me back to my mission.

The road to restoration and recovery was long and not always well lit. I continued to talk openly about my past struggles with friends and family; I believed that was part of the healing process, and I had many apologies to make to many friends and family who had been affected by my spiraling. Most important, I recognized my need to ask for help when I needed that.

All my life, I had struggled on my own or did things myself. It took my hitting bottom to realize that people wanted to help others and that it was satisfying for them to do that. That was a life-changing concept for a guy who had suffered for far too long and had compartmentalized and buried all his feelings—fearful of rejection, damaging his career, and being judged as weak. One of the most amazing gifts given to me by the grace of God was the birth of my twins Blake and Victoria on July 12, 2012. They and their mom were healthy, which is all a proud dad could ever want.

Have you ever laid hold of something? I mean really laid hold of something in your hands that you truly honored? I was the first one to lay hands on my twins. I cut their umbilical cords. I didn't watch from a video or on FaceTime. I had created life again.

I heard my twins take their first lung-squeezing breaths and cry and I laid hands on them before we even knew their names. They gave voice to who I was as a person and how I would approach my life and become the essence of who I was going to be. My spirit, my character, my calling. Not a job, not a gig ... my calling. This was a true gift of my sobriety and naturally gave me a whole new purpose and meaning for the word *grateful*. As every parent can attest to, there is no greater love you will have until you have children. Another gift that was given to me through grace was a reunion with my older brother, Kerry, who had distanced himself from my family for six long years. It was a really nice feeling to reconnect with him and his family without any drama.

I was working hard, enjoying my family, and focusing on being a decent human being again as well as an involved dad, which I had felt guilty about not having been during Isabel's infancy. I knew all this hard work on myself would come back to me in the form of a new mission. And it did.

One Sunday evening in November 2015, the television show *60 Minutes* aired a special about Leslie Stahl's husband's battle with Parkinson's disease. They reported on new research that was sweeping the globe about how boxing but without contact was helping those with Parkinson's reduce their symptoms. The research showed that boxing training protected the dopamine cells from breaking down. This is the chemical neurotransmitter that gives us the gift of movement.

I never watched much television, so I had missed that segment. But four people who had seen it asked me if I had heard about this new breakthrough.

"Brett, I saw this program and the amazing results that people with Parkinson's disease are achieving. I'd love it if you could help my dad before it's too late."

"Brett, did you see the special on Parkinson's and boxing? It's right up your alley. Just let us know if you decide to get involved. My husband is really starting to decline. This could be a lifesaver for him."

"Brett, My dad is ninety, but we think it would bring great quality of life to him to keep moving as best he can. He would love to box with you!"

All who spoke to me about the program had personal connections with Parkinson's and its symptoms' unpredictability. All had family members who suffered horribly from it. They wanted me to watch the show, and they asked when I was going to start doing this style of boxing program in a fitness center. They knew that I was involved in the conditioning of world-champion boxers and that I cornered in professional boxing as a licensed second. The purpose of a cornerman or a second is to coach or assist a fighter during a fight. I told them I would look into it, and I followed through. It was important to me to be accountable, and it was important to them that I respond.

I pulled up the YouTube video from the night before and *Wham!* My new mission came at me like a freight train. I found a video about this inspiring group of people in Brooklyn, New York, who were battling Parkinson's disease through the sport of boxing. The human spirit displayed in the short segment was nothing but miraculous. I listened, and the universe called. I was so lifted by this segment; I wondered why in less than twenty-four hours four people had asked me into their families to help someone they loved. Four people ... twenty-four hours ... The alarm had sounded. It was time. I needed to help them.

I hurried to my research lab—the internet—and started researching all the literature and research about this use of boxing and how to certify myself in this application so I could implement a program at the fitness center where I was teaching other classes. I flew to Indianapolis for three days of intense training learning the boxing technique and some high-intensity training that was behind decreasing symptoms of Parkinson's disease. It has been reported through research that Parkinsons Disease is the fast growing neurological disorder in the world and could possibly be the new pandemic of the 21st century. Parkinson's disease is a movement disorder that affects the central nervous system due to a loss of dopamine in the brain. Treatment is typically based on the array of symptoms one may have including the most common being tremor, rigidity, slow movement, and a loss of balance associated with falls. Unfortunately Parkinson's disease also affects people through non-motor symptoms including insomnia, anxiety, constipation, and depression. The most common medication used is the same medicine used since the sixties. There currently is no cure for Parkinson's disease but the research leads to high intensity interval training exercise to reduce symptoms along with a specific holistic approach of multiple disciplines for the optimum results. Each person with Parkinson's disease is a snowflake and that recipe for maximizing performance is individual to each person.

The training in Indianapolis was emotionally moving, and I was so in my sweet spot. After that first day, I sent videos and called friends about how inspired I was. This is going to be a huge undertaking, and it will be a game changer for people afflicted with this awful disease. I reached out to close friends and people in the boxing business looking for volunteers to help get this project off the ground. My goal from that first day of the training conference was to develop the largest wellness center in the world for Parkinson's disease until a cure was found.

I returned to Massachusetts with my certification as a Rock Steady boxing coach, and I was determined to get this program off the ground. I reached out to people including those who had encouraged me to do something for their loved ones with Parkinson's. I advertised and printed literature and put together some equipment at the fitness center, and voilà—the grand opening occurred on August 16, 2017—my first class.

Alas, only two people showed up with their family members that day. It was not the grand hoopla inspirational class that I had hoped to hold. I had been excited, but like all things, you think everyone knows what you're doing because you're so engrossed in it, but few actually know; I found that out rather painfully.

However, within six months, we had twenty people in our boxing program; our community had begun. Clients traveled from near and far because there was nothing like it in the area. People came from Boston and Cape Cod two sometimes three days a week. We had wonderful volunteers many of whom were family members giving back and others who had heard about our program and wanted to be involved in it.

After a year, we were maxed out of space with about fifty fighters and their families three days a week. By then, we were having impromptu support groups, fundraisers, coffee hours, dinners, and monthly bowling outings.

The universe had called again. The community needed more, and I believed there were hundreds more people with Parkinson's isolated in their homes on the South Shore of Massachusetts not knowing that there was help out there and that they didn't have to be alone again. The universe had saved my life, and it would save theirs.

In November 2016, I found a building that would be the new home of 110 Fitness. This space would be dedicated and named after my military team members, who believed in always performing at a hundred and ten percent. It was often used as a nickname: "Hey One Ten! Want to pack that gear for us?" or as a verb: "One ten that for me, will ya?" I named my business 110 Fitness in homage to my team. I believed in that ethic as much as I believed in them.

The building was a giant, 10,000-square-foot place with a 6,000-square-foot warehouse along with a separate fitness studio, art workshop, and Reiki treatment area. It was an old dishwashing business; when I arrived there, I saw boxes of soap, machinery, hundreds of commercial dishwashers, a fork lift, and metal shelving from ceiling to floor.

It was overwhelming at first. How was I going to convert a dingy, dirty warehouse with oil-stained floors and cobwebs into a premier boxing exercise arena that was welcoming and full of positive energy? I went home trying to imagine all the scenarios I could create in that space and make it functional, optimal, and affordable. Lots of planning, lots of worry, and lots of constant reconfigurations. Geronimo!

It took almost three weeks for the salvage company to clean the warehouse so I could start building my dream space, a place that would accommodate as many people as possible who were struggling with exclusion due to disability or disease. A place that could grow organically from the community in it. The goal was to see the young and the old, the able and disabled, the broken and unbroken merge in a nonjudgmental way and learn from each other.

I took out a large personal loan and ordered almost all my equipment to slowly put this vision together. It took many ten- to twelve-hour workdays with the help of a few volunteers to put most of the heavy equipment up including a twenty-by-twenty-foot boxing ring, barbell weight racks, and heavy bag racks. Everything had its place, and there was plenty of open space to move safely.

I worked through Thanksgiving and Christmas of 2017 to make sure we were ready for a January 3, 2018 grand opening and a seamless transition from our old place to this new place. These folks including the volunteers were so faithful. I wanted no gaps in their training for symptom management purposes. I put the finishing touches on just before New Year's including signage and comfortable furniture for guests and caregivers right down to a train set and coloring books for the kids. We had a meeting with all the employees at my home with a nice progressive meal and reviewed all the schedule and membership details for a smooth crossover.

January 3, 2017—grand opening time! We did a formal ribbon cutting, interviews with the media, and tour after tour after tour, and we had a great turnout. Our Parkinson's family that had followed us from the previous facility, their families, and a whole new group of employees of all disciplines were on the way to making dreams come true and having a solid impact on the lives of people in our community.

We were the first all-inclusive wellness center of this kind; we accepted people of all abilities and disabilities. The next year, we added more and more programming and built networks with established foundations including the Michael J. Fox Foundation, the Davis Phinney Foundation, and the Parkinson's Foundation. I was asked to be an ambassador for two of these foundations as well as a consultant for the Cleveland Clinic.

Our programming—Rock Steady boxing, yoga classes, Pedaling for Parkinson's, cardio kickboxing, and many other classes—served Parkinson's disease and MS patients. We grew to serve youth and adults with disabilities including chronic Lyme disease, Down syndrome, autism, chronic traumatic encephalopathy (CTE), and cerebral palsy. We implemented programming for disabled veterans, the visually impaired, and women afflicted by domestic violence.

Our Parkinson's therapy attendance had grown to over a hundred members, and we became a hotspot for research for the well-known Boston hospitals and universities. We also became the lead research team for new medical devices being introduced to treat Parkinson's symptoms.

Two years later, we celebrated a gala that over five hundred people attended, and we had amazing sponsors and guest speakers. This yearly event funds our scholarship program for people who can't afford our programming—No one is left behind. My 110 Fitness had afforded me meetings, dinners, and conversations with incredibly inspiring people including Yolanda Ali (the wife of Muhammad), Michael J. Fox, Connie and Davis Phinney, Andrea Bocelli and his lovely wife, Jay Alberts, Mick Ebeling, Jimmy Choi (three-time Ninja Warrior with Parkinson's disease), Tim Hague (winner of Canada's Amazing Race with Parkinson's disease), Joan Jett, Christopher Lloyd, Akbar Gbaja-Biamila, and many more in the business of innovation and selflessness for the sake of humanity.

My dream had come true; the 110 Fitness community had become the model program for the universe and the largest wellness center in the world for people with Parkinson's disease. It was time to get to work and figure out how we could shine the light for more wellness programming with professional standards of care and safe, ethical practices across the country and world. And that's what we did.

It's a beautiful day to save lives.

Chapter 13

Getting Off the Ropes

T HE SONG "HALL OF FAME" by The Script has always resonated with me. With its haunting piano intro and rollicking tempo, it's an exhortation to take on the world, to be King Kong thumping your chest, to knock on God's door and talk to him. It's about taking back your power despite any difficulties you might have. It's about round 15, and it's about life. It's the story of a hero, and the hero is you. Stopping when you're finished, not just when you're fatigued. Betting everything you have on yourself with no guarantees at all. Claiming ownership of your experience without letting your past define you. Being the example of the change you want to see in others. Creating influence.

This was the inner music that was playing again in me. Finding a way to offer spiritual, physical, and mental gifts to people rather than material gifts.

This was my new life.

I wanted to represent an idea. I wanted to represent possibilities. I wanted to touch millions of people's lives in hopes that the world would never be the same because I had come into being. In the trenches was where I belonged and where the universe wanted me to be all along. Every story I told you previously indicated this along with my need to give back to my community so I could heal my damaged soul. This new focus brought high intensity and pure concentration that consumed all my energy and permeated my existence.

With this new mission and a new life with less struggle, the picture became clearer and clearer for me; I saw what valuable lessons I was to remain teachable for. I started to surround myself with this strong, unshakeable community. We went out to the margins and found the sick, the suffering, and the voiceless and brought them into our circle. Those for whom the armor had become too heavy and those who no longer had a mission. We rose together against the mental warfare of Parkinson's disease with support groups for families and their children along with providing a safe, nonjudgmental place where people weren't defined by their diseases or disabilities.

As Father Greg Boyle, founder of Homeboy Industries, says, when you go out to the margins, if you listen carefully, you can hear angels singing. I can attest to that. It's so beautiful. It's like a sound you'd never heard before that is so peaceful and heavenly. Father Boyle said that when you go to the margins, don't go to save people but to savor them. They will teach you what you can achieve. Create a circle of compassion where everyone is included and no one is left behind.

In my restorative recovery, something I learned besides being able to ask for help was to remain humble and teachable, and this is what I learned working in the trenches on the margins.

Every day, wake up and make the decision to be a daily hero. The world needs as many as it can get. You might be the teacher who shows a child how to read, a single parent who teaches his or her child how to tie shoes, a coach who teaches disabled adults how to hit a speed bag two times in a row, or a caregiver who spoon-feeds her dad at a nursing home. We are all daily heroes. Congrats!

As a human being, you have a certain power whether you know it or not; every person you've ever come in contact with, every place you've ever visited, and every space you've ever occupied was changed because you were there. I know what you're thinking: *No one asked me if I wanted all that power. That's a whole lot of responsibility I didn't sign up for.* My simple answer to that is that no one asked Peter Parker if he wanted to be Spider-Man; he happened to be bitten by a spider, and you happened to be born. It's your job to save the day every day and take care of those around you. The harder you work to make this life worth living for everyone, the better this life will be.

In the words of Sue Monk Kidd, "There is no place so awake and alive as the edge of becoming. But more than that, being the kind of person who can authentically say my soul is my own and then embody it in their life in their spirituality and in their community. It's worth the risk and the hardship."(Kidd, Sue Monk. *The Dance of the Dissident Daughter*. HarperOne, 2016.

Live on the edge of becoming, and know it's worth the risk. Know your whys and what fors. Dive into the FFTs (effin' first times) as Dr. Brené Brown would say, and know how hard it is to be new at things. Vulnerability is courageous as hell. Feel the fear—and do it anyway. Be brave in uncertainty, and step up to the commitment the universe has signed you up for. Show up!

When I went out to the margins, we found daily heroes already doing their part who were there to help us recognize more of our purpose. They were there to nurture and foster more- effective ways to use our powers and redefine our mission. We savored them; we didn't save them.

The take-home here was that my life would play out for me as it had been destined since I was seven, a plan well laid out by the universe including victories, struggles, humility, and regeneration. We all have these phases of life in different orders and repetitions. We need to steadfastly recognize and embrace them for the universe has tasked all of us to help others and our communities and consequently to help ourselves stay in and on our mission.

Life on life's terms we call it—being accountable, being responsible, and being grateful. Tasking ourselves with helping others who in turn help many. Not rearranging the entire world but helping heal the part of the world that's in our reach. Our goal should be to assist each other body to body causing a large, massive tipping of the earth's goodness. This empathy and soul-sharing creates influence and drastic change by adding and adding until there's so much accumulation of acts of kindness. We don't know nor are we to know where our act plays in this tipping process—we know only that it's part of the process. Injecting light into our communities during times of darkness or during times of need one soul at a time, and showing mercy to others; these are small acts of intense bravery and great necessity.

Spend each day as if it's your whole lifetime. Never put your interests above the team or the mission because you will fail miserably especially if you are the leader of the mission. Being a part of and contributing to the overall mission of yourself or a group, you'll start to see your life as an opportunity to share your special power that you alone can spread across the world.

You are enough!

Whether you're the single mother of an autistic child and elderly parents, or the eighty-five-year-old caregiver of a spouse who gets up ten times a night and has hallucinations, or the young soldier in a wheelchair who has lost an extremity and is riddled with anxiety, everyone can do his or her part; everyone can help another person.

It's been my privilege to do the universe's work and be presented with situations in which I could use my skills and healing power. Having those skills and abilities was a good thing. My mental health had devolved into anxiety, hyper-alertness, and emotional detachment and created an internal struggle fully stunting my personal growth, but it was worth the constant brain simmer. My existence is now so much more defined and the intricacy of my life purpose so much clearer because of it.

I will dedicate the duration of my life to giving back to the margins and my community of broken but still colorful crayons—people with movement disorders, people without movement disorders, disabled kids, kids with chronic diseases, disabled adults, young adults on the spectrum, elite athletes with CTE and concussions, disabled veterans, people in recovery, and people afflicted by trauma of all fashions. I don't see them as broken people; I see them as beautiful humans capable of a range of colors and tints and hues of accomplishment and drive. My 110 Fitness will continue to be an all-inclusive wellness center where everyone is welcome and no one is excluded.

If you're broken and damaged but still kicking some ass, we believe in you, and we want you to come share yourself with us. Because of the amazing community we've created, 110 Fitness's vibration and energies have brought together the most kind, brave, consistent, considerate, human-spirited volunteers (corner people). They are the nuts and bolts of our programming. They all have reached a new level of consciousness from positive feedback loops and have intentionality back in their lives through the good work they are doing through our members. They have all been touched, moved, and inspired by some of the strongest humans ever.

I have the honor of watching people every day who have chronic diseases, disabilities, or movement disorders who never give up. They show up daily and put in the work needed to literally save their lives. They trudge in for an hour of intense exercise though they hadn't wanted even to get out of bed. They get the gift of movement through the coaching and encouragement of our volunteers and their fellow comrades.

The story begins at 110 Fitness for our volunteers of rebirth, restoration, and regeneration of life's true mission for them. Finding the gift or super power that only they as individuals can offer to the world. We had achieved the truest form of humanity in our community. Helping one, helping many.

It's a beautiful way to save lives.

Chapter 14

The Looping Effect: Meeting Arik

THE LOOPING EFFECT OF LIFE is an amazing concept and one that presented itself to me in the most mysterious way in the fall of 2019. Life again brought me a powerful reminder that gratefulness in its purest form is present and abundant in people you may have saved but never even knew. The looping effect hit me hard when I met Arik. Some might say when I met him for the second time.

September 2019 was a cherished time for our family as my niece was getting married and we would be heading to Pennsylvania for a beautiful weekend wedding in cow country. That gave us an opportunity to see my brother, his wife, and my other nieces and nephews. My wife and I weren't much for staying in hotels, and we wanted to make our trip with our children a little more of an adventure, so we planned in a mini vacation on a farm near Amish country.

By chance, we got the last room at Rocky Acre Farm, one of the largest dairy farms in the United States that also had a giant farm house for people to stay at and enjoy farm life for a weekend. Our suite was decorated with beautiful fieldstone walls, a loft for my twins to sleep in, and country decor from the oversized log cabin–style windows to the lacy shower curtain.

Per their webpage, we found out that our kids would be able to feed newborn calves and gather eggs from the hen house. The farm had miniature horses to ride, goats to pet, and kittens to cuddle. Our family would love Rocky Acre Farm! It had been designed for kids our age. Amazing views, lots of history, and lots of home-cooked farm food.

Rocky Acre Farm turned out to be all of that and more for my family and especially for me. The universe's plan again.

The Miller family piled into the van late one Thursday afternoon after work and school for the eight-hour drive to Mt. Joy, Pennsylvania. The twins had their books, DVDs, snacks, favorite stuffed animals, and blankets. Road trips for kids nowadays are sure different from what they were when we were kids. We drove through Rhode Island, Connecticut, over the GW bridge in rush hour (*Yeehaw!*) into Jersey and finally into Pennsylvania. I drove long, dark, twisting farm roads in the back country and scanned constantly for deer as we drove down the corn-filled corridors.

We arrived at 11:30 that night; we had called ahead, but no one had answered. We hoped someone would be there to greet us. The kids were sound asleep. We drove up a hilly driveway and approached the front door. It was dark and spooky. *Bang bang bang!* I pounded on the door. No one answered. We saw a small light on in one room. *Bang bang bang!* Still no one. Our excitement about the weekend started to dwindle. We headed back to the car to call again in hopes we could get in touch with someone. Suddenly, the door whipped open, and a short, plump, and adorable older woman yelled, "You must be the Millers. Please come in. We've been waiting on ya."

In her nighty and slippers, Eileen Benner welcomed us in. She turned out to be a night owl and a talkative one at that. We started talking, and we found out that she too was a Miller (her family name), and we also heard the farm's schedule and vitamin regimen for this, healthy, eighty-five-year young woman, who with her husband, Galen, owned one of the largest dairy farms in the United States. It never felt so good to lie our heads down that night after all the travel and the late-night gossip.

Morning would come too quickly—5:00 a.m.!—with our children excited to be at the farm and of course the roosters calling. It was as beautiful in the daylight as it was on the internet. Stillness, sun rising, cows mooing, chickens crowing, and acres of dewy corn fields as far as the eye could see. Sometimes, being awake earlier than you wanted to be in such a peaceful place outweighs your sensation of fatigue and brings pure relaxation.

I was excited about seeing the farm's eight hundred acres after the country breakfast the farm had boasted about in its advertisements. We washed up, dressed, and headed downstairs to chow, and it did not disappoint—everything you could imagine and more. Eileen was pulling a shoofly pie out of the oven. It was a breakfast I will never forget, but it wasn't just because of the food.

We ate at a table with twenty-foot benches on each side, and all the places were full. Eileen invited our family to eat with her at the kitchen table with another couple and their two children. She dominated the conversation with all kinds of great stories of wisdom and things to do on the farm that day. She was so excited to meet another Miller family.

My dad's family was from the Poconos, so I was sure there was some distant crossover along the family tree somewhere. The young couple across from us was very intent on listening and participating in the conversation, but when they spoke to each other, it was in another language. The syllables were guttural and unclear, and the accent was strong but strangely familiar. It had been a long time, but it was an accent and language I had never forgotten. I had flashbacks of playing marbles with children in the streets of Macedonia and Bosnia during my military missions in the late nineties.

I whispered to my wife, "Do you hear that?"

"Hear what?"

"They're Bosnians!"

My wife had met me long after I had retired from the army and was clearly not impressed that I knew their language and heritage. She probably thought I would be coming up with some smart-ass comment about it. And by the look on her face, she also couldn't believe that I was being so rude whispering at a table full of people.

I was fascinated and happily surprised all at the same time because it had been twenty-one years since I had seen someone from Bosnia, and there I was at a table with a Bosnian family. It was brilliant! In my typical hyper-alert state, I watched the dynamics of the family. They were so loving and polite while I was planning my attack for the post-breakfast introduction. I didn't want to scare them; they were on vacation as we were, and they would be surely taken back by some random guy diving into the depths of a conversation with a group of people who clearly had a scarred past. For that matter, they may have been born here in the United States as citizens and not really have known the history of one of the most unspoken about and less-known human tragedies.

I indulged in the wonderful country breakfast with my family and these wonderful people including Eileen. We talked about our families and where we were living and how we had ended up at Rocky Acre Farm; we were making familiar connections in one way or another as humans do. The kids were planning their animal visits and hayrides for the day. Three families, three generations, three different walks of life, and three different heritages all at one table immersed in each other without judgment and with love. Imagine that! What an amazing concept! Mind-blowing yet so fulfilling for our souls and for my children to bear witness to something so beautiful with no preemptive thoughts.

A lot of this tragedy was never spoken about to the majority of the world. I was fortunate enough to be a part of this history after most of the mass murder and genocide had occurred. As I spoke about in a previous chapter, I had been a military consultant who helped develop more-efficient evacuations of injured and maimed adults and children refugees from Bosnia as well as implementing more-effective acute medical care in Skopje, Macedonia, which inadvertently became a postwar safe zone for triage.

Seeing the awful effects of the purge while in Bosnia when I was a soldier had been bad enough. Even as a nonparticipant, it added to my PTSD. But then as a parent and having seen truckloads of families split apart, injured, and having lost their loved ones and their homes, I couldn't even wrap my head around the feelings of those hundreds of thousands of refugees left with nothing but the clothes they were wearing.

The scarred landscape of Macedonia and the scarred people I encountered there were in sharp contrast to the charming scene on the farm—from rocks, desert, and war-torn rubble to grassy pastures, contented animals, and growing crops. It was a mind-blower.

After such a wonderful breakfast, the festivities on the farm commenced. It was the time of year that the combines were harvesting corn and dumping it into big trucks. Galen, pulled out his big old tractor for a hayride through the dairy farm. All the kids were in heaven watching these massive machines at work. We all piled in the trailer full of hay bales; my kids were sitting with the kids from the breakfast table probably because they looked familiar. It was a different type of hayride that day because all the kids were experiencing scenery they had never seen before including thousands of cows—and I mean thousands—and silos as high as the sky, rows of combines chewing up corn like lawn mowers, and fields as far as the eye could see. The whole tour was directed by Galen, who had grown up on this farm and was passing it down to his kids as a third-generation dairy farm.

Ironically, on Miller Street, under the covered bridge on the west side of the farm, we saw multiple Amish folks in horse-drawn buggies. We returned to the farmhouse after the tour, and the kids were ready to run off together to see the barn kittens and all the calves that had been born the night before. My kids were playing with the Bosnian kids, and I knew this was my chance to introduce myself.

I headed over to the kids when the Bosnian gentleman was walking with me as our kids were together. He was an athletic, unassuming, quiet guy in his mid- to late thirties. Hair unbrushed, and his face two to three days unshaven. He was enjoying the day as I was seeing our children so happy and relaxed.

"This place is amazing," I said. "Quite an operation. Are you on vacation?"

"Yes. We arrived last night. Our kids are loving the farm life," he replied in that heavily accented voice.

I'm sure he thought that I was just some fast-talking Bostonian with my own heavy accent. I told him that my niece was getting married and that instead of staying in a hotel, we thought we would give our children this experience. I also shared with him that my brother had lived in Mt. Joy, Pennsylvania, for many years having moved from Massachusetts. "How about you?" I asked.

"We're on a family vacation from upstate New York. This is the second year in a row we've been here. The kids love it."

"Nice. I spent one of the coldest winters of my life for two weeks in Upstate New York at Fort Drum in Utica. Are you that far up?"

"Yes. We live right near there."

106

"I couldn't help but note your accent. Were you born in the United States? Or are you from Yugoslavia?"

Clearly a bit surprised, he turned to me. "Not many people would recognize my accent. I'm surprised you picked up on it. I'm from Sarajevo. I moved here with my brother and my parents when I was eight."

I thought he might have been a refugee who had escaped the 1995 genocide, but I am sure he would've explained that. It seemed that his parents had decided to move to the United States for a better life for him and his brother as so many families had back then.

"My name is Brett by the way."

"Arik. Good to meet you."

Our kids were pulling on the ear tags of the calves and feeding them straw, just loving their soft, velvety hides.

"Do you remember what year you left Sarajevo? Do you still have family there?"

I felt a little too aggressive with my conversation, but I'd never really known after that mess of a war involving so many politics, religions, and opinions if what we had done for those people as soldiers of the United States military had made a difference. It was a piece of my life that had no closure but many horrific memories of ethnic cleansing and displaced families. I was hoping for some validation because I selfishly needed to close that door some twenty-two years later.

I tried to explain. "I was in Bosnia a couple of years after the genocide as a US Army medic. We were trying to help the government streamline evacuations and care for the refugees and injured people." I just stared at him. He seemed hesitant to answer my questions or perhaps wasn't able to answer because I was asking so many questions so quickly. I waited with ears open and eyes peeled like a dog on a bone.

What seemed like a slow minute clicked by. Still silence. He looked at me and took a deep breath; he was processing all I had said. Tears began rolling down his face. He looked right into my eyes and deep into my soul and said, "Thank you. You saved my family's lives."

I was speechless.

Arik and I sat on a hay bale in the middle of a farm in the middle of Mt. Joy, Pennsylvania, watching our kids play so innocently. He told me his story of being an eight-year-old in Bosnia. "My family survived the massacre of Srebrenica in 1995."

Arik spoke with care and emotion; it must have been hard for him to talk about what he and his family had been through. I let him talk.

"When our door was busted open one night, we assumed we would all be shot by rebels. But they were US soldiers. They snatched up my parents, my brother, and me and took us to a refugee camp in Tuzla. We spent a couple of nights sleeping outside with just our clothes to keep us warm. The next day, we were processed and shipped to New York. We were issued an empty apartment in the Bronx and given a stipend that was barely enough to feed us. And we spoke no English." He sighed and looked away clearly lost in his memories. He said softly, "We used to walk the streets of the Bronx on trash pickup days to look for furniture for our apartment."

All the pictures in my mind, all the people I had interacted with, and all the scenarios I had encountered in Bosnia and the surrounding countries ran through my mind as I listened to Arik tell his inspiring story of resilience. My heart was pounding. It was terrible to see the results and hear about it. Being a parent made this story harder to hear and tell, I'm sure.

"So what did your parents do?" I asked.

"They found people who hired them, and they learned English at their jobs. My brother and I were left at home to take care of each other."

"Are they still alive? That is really an impressive story." I couldn't imagine being plopped down in a foreign country not knowing the language, the money, the work regulations ... It was mind-boggling.

"Yeah, my brother and I grew up and became citizens, and we relocated to an established Bosnian culture in upstate New York. My parents live with me, my wife, and my children. All the businesses in town are owned by people who had been refugees, and we all speak the same language. It's really cool."

Giving back as a young man for all his parents had sacrificed and had done for him and his brother. It was very common for European families to reside together.

Most people would not have been grateful, but Arik's family was grateful to not be hiding in their homes anymore waiting to be raped or murdered. Grateful to be given an opportunity to survive. Arik was poised and proud of his culture and his family as he told his emotional story. His mom and dad wasted no time making a life worth being proud of for their children. They worked hard, learned English on their own, and brought their children up with a strong work ethic and values.

As I listened to Arik's story, I thought of the emotional and psychological toll it must have taken on his family to have been uprooted from a country they had called home. Horrifying.

Arik said that he had met his wife in his community, where thousands of refugees had relocated to after settling in the United States. Bosnian business owners brought together a large gathering of this community who played soccer daily as the sport was so prevalent in Europe as well. He paused for a long second; I think he was reflecting on all that had just happened.

Arik thanked me again for my military service and all that we had done as soldiers to help the innocent men, women, and children of his country. Most important, he reminded me that whether I knew it or not, it had been a beautiful day to save lives in Bosnia in 1996 for a twenty-three-year-old army medic named Brett.

Arik and I were thousands of miles from the war zone where we'd first had our paths cross. Leaving the rocky grit and torn soil of Bosnia for this living, breathing, life-giving farm was a journey beyond mere miles. It was a journey of our souls.

That idyllic morning, we watched our children playing together with those farm animals, and we laughed and cried for all the reasons you could imagine. Two men from different countries with different childhoods sitting together in arms as brothers. Proud of our families, proud of our heritage, and proud of our accomplishments despite the hardships we had faced. I'm not sure who saved whom that day. The synchronicity and the universe's timing of that event was all I needed to validate that I was on the right path in life. I knew that there was something greater than all of us called the universe, and it sure had a very specific plan that day.

Although my battlefield is different now, I continue to make humanity my responsibility. My new battlefield is consumed with righteous purpose, not by heavy armor. Trying to do the next right thing for the sake of humanity and with positive intentions. Every day is a beautiful day to save lives, and that is my universal-given gift. I have also realized that it doesn't have to be in the midst of a crisis; a simple act of kindness can change and even save someone's life.

What's your universal gift? Whatever it may be, recognize it, get after it, and share it with the world. Greatness is upon you, and you better act on it.

It's always a beautiful day to save lives.

Godspeed, and God bless America!

My long-lost friend Arik

Resources

These information sources focus on Parkinson's disease, veterans' resources, and foundations that help patients.

- 110 Fitness—www.110fitness.org. 781-616-3313. bmiller@110fitness.org
- 22kill.com
- APDA—www.apdaparkinson.org. 800-223-2732.
- Davis Phinney Foundation—www.davisphinneyfoundation. org. 866-358-0285.
- Michael J. Fox Foundation—www.michaeljfox.org. 800-708-7644.
- Parkinson's Foundation—www.parkinson.org. 800-473-4636.
- Veterans' Crisis Line—800-273-8255.

Deep human connection is the purpose and the result of a meaningful life—and it will inspire the most amazing acts of love, generosity, and humanity.

—Melinda Gates

About the Author

Brett is passionate about adaptive fitness and inspiring the best in everyone he meets. The mission of his wellness design is to set a new standard for the world in the "fight back" against Parkinson's Disease through holistic and fitness based approaches as well as breaking down all barriers for adults and children limited by disease or disability by sharing his exceptional mental and physical training and conditioning experience

Brett is a licensed physical therapist with 26 years of experience in all settings including sports therapy, acute and intensive care, long-term care, and wound care. He has worked in the fitness industry for over 26 years with extensive experience in adaptive fitness, kickboxing, boxing, spinning, rowing, and strength and conditioning. He is the Founder and Owner of 110 Fitness and the Head Coach of Rock Steady Boxing South Shore. He has worked as the strength and conditioning coach for world-class boxers and Olympic athletes focusing on injury prevention and rehabilitation. Additionally, he is the co-owner and operator of Boston Orthotics, Inc. for the past 17 years. Brett was also an adaptive sports coach at New England Disabled Sports at Loon Mountain in Lincoln, New Hampshire for 18 years.

Brett is a U.S. Army veteran and is proud to have served as a combat medic trainer for special operations and oversaw the construction and development of the DEPMEDS for the United States Army. Brett is a PWR!Moves® Certified Therapist. Brett is also certified in Concept 2 Rowing, Pedaling for Parkinson's, SCW Boxing Fitness, SCW Aquatics Exercise, Tai Ji Quan: Moving for Better Balance, CPR/AED, and is a licensed boxing second in the state of Massachusetts. Brett also serves as an ambassador for the Michael J. Fox Foundation for Parkinson's

Research and the Davis Phinney Foundation. Brett is also a research consultant for innovative United States research companies as well as prominent Boston hospitals and the Cleveland Clinic.

Brett resides in Hanson, Massachusetts with his lovely wife Audrey, their oldest daughter, Isabel, and their twins, Blake and Victoria.